Praise for *Cross Cultures: Change Across Generations*

I am very excited about Dennis Jaffe's and Jim Grubman's book, *Cross Cultures*. Their book contains a comprehensive discussion of cultural anthropology that our field has long needed but which, until now, has not been available to families and their advisors. The authors offer clear descriptions of each of the three principal cultural types on our planet, of how families behave and make decisions within each culture, and most importantly, why they do. They help us understand how profoundly different decision-making is in each culture. Having been professionally engaged with families in all three cultures, I can say my experience mirrors everything the authors say and so much more that I didn't understand. I wish I had had this book to guide me in my career.

> James (Jay) E. Hughes, Jr., Author of *Family Wealth: Keeping It in the Family* and co-author of *Family Trusts: A Guide for Beneficiaries, Trustees, Trust Protectors, and Trust Creators*

This ground-breaking book uses new research on culture and negotiation to assist families and family businesses. Jaffe and Grubman translate important concepts to help families understand and manage the cultural transitions underlying the generational transitions that stress the fabric of family life and viability of family businesses.

> Jeanne M. Brett, DeWitt W. Buchanan, Jr. Distinguished Professor of Dispute Resolution and Organizations, Kellogg School of Management, Northwestern University, and author of *Negotiating Globally, 3rd Edition*

This insightful work contributes valuable concepts regarding the Journey Up and the Journey Across cultures for families. The book clearly defines the global citizen with a multi-cultural perspective who blends values from the home culture with the new culture where schooling occurs. The authors close by saying it best: "By treating generational issues as partly cultural, families are able to frame issues and negotiate solutions in highly adaptive ways." *Cross Cultures* gives you keen insight for navigating that journey.

> Sara Hamilton, Founder and CEO, Family Office Exchange

This is an excellent and timely book contributing to the greater understanding of all cultures, essential to preserving global peace and prosperity as we march towards the 22nd Century.

> Roger King, PhD, Director, Tanoto Center for Asian Business and Entrepreneurship Studies, Hong Kong University of Science and Technology

Cross Cultures

Cross Cultures

HOW GLOBAL FAMILIES NEGOTIATE CHANGE ACROSS GENERATIONS

Dennis T. Jaffe PhD
and James Grubman PhD

Copyright © 2016 FamilyWealth Consulting

All rights reserved. No part of this publication may be reproduced, distributed, or transmitted in any form or by any means, including photocopying, recording, or other electronic or mechanical methods, without the prior written permission of the publisher, except in the case of brief quotations embodied in critical reviews and certain other noncommercial uses permitted by copyright law.

Printed in the United States of America

Jaffe, Dennis and Grubman, James.
Cross Cultures: How Global Families Negotiate Change Across Generations / Dennis Jaffe and James Grubman.

ISBN-10: 1517626609
ISBN-13: 978-1517626600

Book Design: VJB/Scribe
Cover art: Michael Chen

To the extended Jaffe-Scott clan, including our parents and grandparents, along with our children and grandchildren who carry on our wonderful legacy

—Dennis Jaffe

To my incredible family, especially my grandchildren. They truly are the future.

—James Grubman

Contents

Foreword by Barbara Hauser   ix
Acknowledgments   xi

1. Introduction   1

I
The Three Global Cultures

2. Surveying the Landscape: Understanding Culture   13
3. The Three Global Cultures   21
4. Individualist Culture   29
5. Collective Harmony Culture   37
6. Honor Culture   49
7. Comparison of the Three Cultural Styles   57

II
The Journey Up, the Journey Across

8. The Journey Up   63
9. The Journey Up in the Three Cultures   71
10. The Journey Across   79

III
Negotiating Change Across Generations

11. Negotiating the Family's Future   99
12. The Process of Negotiating Change   109
13. The Advisor as Cultural Mediator   121
14. Thriving in the Global Landscape   133

Appendix: Basics of Family Governance   139

Notes   *142*
About the Authors   *148*

Foreward

By Barbara Hauser

YOU ARE IN FOR A TREAT!

Dennis Jaffe and Jim Grubman have very thoughtfully analyzed the single biggest weakness in current approaches to the issue of family wealth "longevity." Governance advice for families needs to be rethought in light of their insights. That central weakness is the unexamined Western cultural background implicit in most accepted advice—even by those advisors who are not part of Western culture themselves.

For example, current advisor recommendations almost always assume that better and more open communication, with all individual views expressed and considered, will lead to stronger and longer-lasting family cohesion. As Jaffe and Grubman persuasively demonstrate, this is a bias of only one world culture (Individualism). There are two other important cultures (Honor and Collective Harmony) that are just as important for many families. Giving advice from one of the three systems to a different system does not work well. Families are confused and advisors cannot understand what went wrong.

The three cultures are described, with a number of examples:

Individualist culture: Western culture including the United States, Canada, Great Britain, Northern Europe and Australia

Collective Harmony culture: East Asian culture, including China, Hong Kong, Singapore, Korea, and Japan

Honor culture: A diverse ethnic cluster consisting of Latin America, Southern Europe, Middle East, India, and Africa

Their analysis adds one level more in sophistication. Families in each of the three cultures, to be successful for multiple generations, will be in a journey "Up" and also "Across." The "Up" is the economic rise from wherever the economic start was, proceeding into the new culture of "wealth." The "Across" is the inevitable spread into and contact with other global contexts. Again, there is a very clear and helpful mapping of these effects. Finally they also add the family dynamics overlay.

As interesting (and as well-researched) as their detailed analysis is in the first parts of the book, the last part is the section that advisors and families will refer to again and again. It contains very practical and specific advice on how to deal with standard procedures and accepted governance elements — when the family's culture and their particular journey are understood. They list a blueprint for a new, more successful approach. My own experience with all three cultures reinforces the value of their outstanding analysis.

Thank you to Dennis and Jim for this major contribution to the field.

Acknowledgments

MANY INSIGHTFUL FRIENDS AND COLLEAGUES HAVE OFFERED IDEAS on this challenging topic. We especially want to thank our wonderful colleagues Kevin Au, Peter Begalla, Jeremy Cheng, Alan Cohen, Justin Craig, Ramia El Agamy, Sasha Grinberg, Sara Hamilton, Barbara Hauser, Lee Hausner, Jay Hughes, Richard Joyner, Roger King, Annie Koh, Isabelle Lescent-Giles, Joshua Nacht, Edgar Schein, Caroline Seow, Suzanne Slater, Ruth Steverlynck, Christian Stewart, Edouard Thijssen, Jamie Traeger-Muney, Matt Wesley, and Yuelin Yang for their thoughtful comments as the book unfolded.

Jeanne Brett very graciously responded to our cold-calling her via email to arrange a meeting which was a true joy. She subsequently contributed valuable perspectives on cultures and negotiation strategies as well as the overall structure of the book. We also thank Erin Meyer of INSEAD for her permission to reference and adapt her cultural dimension scales which are so illuminating.

We are grateful to Valerie Brewster for her last-minute help on the interior and exterior book designs and formatting, and to Michael Chen for his stirring image of the Myanmar boatman.

We especially want to recognize Susan Eckstrom for her patience, hard work, cheerful diligence, and tireless efforts on virtually every aspect of the project. We thank her deeply for her help on the manuscript, graphics, and publication project, including corralling both of us when necessary and maintaining our equilibrium at so many points along the way.

Finally, we each wish to express our deep gratitude to our respective wives, Cynthia Scott and Jeanne Grubman, who provide loving support each day. We are deeply grateful to them for their wisdom, their counsel, and their feedback. They know us well.

CHAPTER 1

Introduction

Heraclitus, the great Greek philosopher, once wrote "character is destiny." It may be said that, in families, culture is destiny. The past and present cultures of a family form the landscape upon which family members put down roots, expand, periodically battle, and pursue happiness. Some families see possibility beyond the cultures of their heritage, migrating to places with richer opportunity. What they encounter, and how successfully they adapt, will shape their destiny for generations to come.

Culture as a Growing Theme in Business and Family

Within the past two decades, there has been an explosion of interest and research about the role of culture in business, psychology, communication, organizational functioning, and negotiation. The tremendous rise in global enterprise has fueled this interest. A modern company may have headquarters in London, factories in China, distribution centers in Brazil and Romania, and markets on four continents. Its management must understand how to integrate, negotiate with, and lead its employees in a multicultural world.

In parallel fashion, a family originating in one culture may develop enterprises and raise children and grandchildren in new locales while simultaneously retaining close ties with their country of origin. Today, most successful business families operate in more than one cultural environment as they spread throughout the world, assimilate into new communities, and build their enterprises.

Cultures in different regions of the world give rise to varied patterns that influence the behavior of business families as they interweave personal relationships, childrearing, and commerce. Understanding family enterprises through the lens of culture allows new insights into a family's nature, its progress or stagnation, and its chances of success for the future. As Jeanne Brett, a renowned specialist in cross-cultural negotiation, has stated:

> Culture is the unique character of a group. Individuals have personalities; groups have cultures. You can see culture in the pattern of people's beliefs, attitudes, norms, and behaviors as well as in the nature of the social, economic, political, legal and religious institutions that structure and organize groups. Anthropologists suggest that culture emerges because people are faced repeatedly with similar social problems.[1]

This fundamental premise—that family enterprises are faced with common, expected, even predictable social stresses over the course of generations—illuminates why understanding culture is so valuable. By expanding the lens and taking the broadest possible perspective, many seemingly idiosyncratic conflicts within family enterprises come into focus as natural developmental transitions within the shifting (or conflicting) cultures within a family.

With fresh perspective also come innovative solutions. New answers emerge to deal with the impasses that arise in family enterprises: stalemates over leadership transitions, fights over maintaining tradition versus embracing change, clashes over marriage partners or inheritance or management of wealth. When families comprehend that their challenges are neither painfully unique nor insurmountable, they gain confidence for the journey ahead.

The Value for Advisors

Understanding the role of culture is also critical for the advisors who work alongside family enterprises. Without perspective on cultural aspects of family wealth and family enterprise, advisors may make important errors that impact the family's success. The various options and perspectives of different generations in a family may arise from different cultural influences rather than from their inclinations as individuals.

Advisors may interpret decisions by wealth creators as reflecting individual personality when those decisions are actually very common for the client's ethnic culture. Conversely, advisors may fail to question or evaluate a family leader's decisions because the advisor shares the same culture and thinks the same way. Neither the wealth creator nor his or her advisors may understand the full menu of options available.

Applying cultural understanding can dramatically increase an advisor's perspective, skills, and effectiveness in helping families face the challenges of wealth and success.

Diversifying Cultural Perspectives about Family Enterprise

Although culture is increasingly recognized as fundamental to family firms worldwide, important concepts have not yet been integrated into an understanding of what happens to families across generations — why some families adapt and succeed while others stagnate or turn upon themselves in unproductive conflict.

One problem is that much of the family business consulting field is Western-centric. Key principles, developed by American thought leaders from the early days of the field, have been extended around the world in recent decades through the increasing influence of international consultants, research institutes, family business centers, and the hard work of consultant practitioners. Organizations such as the Family Firm Institute (FFI), the Family Business Network, and STEP (with its recently-formed Family Business special interest group) are extending the field globally.

Many historically Western concepts do work successfully as best practices for family enterprises across cultures. Global family businesses have benefited enormously from increased understanding about basic tenets of governance structures (e.g., family councils, boards of directors) and procedures (e.g., policy development, family constitutions), as well as the qualities of successful leadership in family enterprises (see the Appendix for a brief description of family governance concepts and terms).

Yet, some Western best practices do not transfer well to other cultures.

How We May React to — and Misunderstand — Different Cultural Behaviors

After spending days working with a Chinese family on shared family values, agreements about forming a family council, and guidelines on family employment and leadership transition, an experienced consultant from the United States was winding up the meeting. He was feeling quite successful in empowering the next generation and the family as a whole. Then, virtually with hand on doorknob, the eldest son mentioned, "Of course, Dad will have a veto over our decisions." The Western consultant was deeply shocked. He felt that all of the family's hard work had just been undermined and rejected. Yet, to his surprise, nobody in the family seemed to feel this was anything but natural.

The consultant gradually realized that, in Chinese culture, the father is eternally in charge of the family, even as his children take on more authority in the business. The unspoken, indirect message to the father in this meeting was "we respect you and acknowledge you for allowing us to take this huge step forward." Equally unspoken was that the father would, in his role as benevolent leader, never invoke his veto power without cause. The consultant was learning that Western-oriented models of family governance might look very different in other cultures in the world.

In developing the new perspectives outlined in this book, we were surprised by how much our consulting work always made certain presumptions common to the field. For example, we generally assumed that, as families cross generations, there is a preference for the personal growth of individual family members to take precedence over deepening of the family collective. The nature of life is for children to grow up and leave the nest, is it not? Staying sheltered in an ever-crowded nest risks stifling individuality and autonomy, those cherished values in Western society.

We missed important ways in which the assumption does not apply well in non-Western cultures. We now know that Western ideas about individuation in families are much more complicated and influenced by cultural changes when applied to global family enterprises.

Other family business consulting principles are also infused with core assumptions and recommendations from a Western perspective:

- open direct communication and transparency
- individual basis for trust
- assertive discussion
- detailed logical analysis
- multiple governance models

Application of these assumptions and procedures does not always go smoothly or effectively when applied to other cultures. Families in strongly authority-based or collective cultures hesitate to adopt common family business recommendations which advocate open communication, shared leadership, directly assertive confrontation, and analytical thinking — all associated with Western thought and action. Despite the field's accepted wisdom, these practices are neither culturally universal nor automatically helpful outside Western culture.

How can a Chinese third-generation family member even approach the patriarch to inquire about the family's succession plan when, in doing so, according to Confucian principles, the patriarch will feel challenged and dishonored? In a Middle-Eastern family where communication must remain indirect and leadership traditionally passes to the eldest son, how can a second-generation daughter (trained at the London School of Economics) broach the idea she wants to be included in the family's next-generation planning? Western concepts about governance, succession, leadership, and communication cannot be layered onto all families around the globe like wallpapering the family home in the fashion of a New York apartment.

Good Intentions, Disappointing Outcome

In a research interview, a thirty-five-year-old Lebanese next-generation family member described a painful experience about the failure of the family's work with a US-based consultant:

"...We even wrote a constitution for the family with a consultant. Before that, we had a weekend discussion and I thought it was going to take us somewhere. But again, somehow when I proposed a draft of the constitution that the consultant had written and I had commented on, they didn't accept it at all. They said, 'we don't need all this.' They were very dismissive, actually. They were very dismissive and negative and basically they felt it was Anglo-Saxon hocus-pocus and they said, 'we don't need this. This is too formal. This is too serious. Who do you think we are?' They took it very badly and I was very disappointed, obviously."[2]

A New Set of Perspectives

The new perspective detailed in this book places Western culture in context as just one of several cultures influencing families. We propose a modern, flexible, integrated model that incorporates the diverse cultural factors present in family enterprises around the world. This innovative perspective, grounded in the latest insights in cross-cultural psychology and organizational functioning, explains more of what works, what doesn't, and why. It also points to actionable recommendations more likely to help families achieve success across generations.

Our model underscores the importance of two major transitions experienced by successful family enterprises, anywhere in the world:

> *The Journey Up*—the fundamental transition in *economic* culture families experience as they emerge from economic adversity and migrate upwards to wealth, success, and affluence.

> *The Journey Across*—the transition in *ethnic* culture that families experience as success leads them to the blend of attitudes, behaviors, and perspectives that is modern global affluence. This "ambicultural blend"[3] incorporates strong elements of Western culture but is infused with elements that are more collective, interdependent, and globally aware than straightforward Western culture.

These two major cultural transitions in the life of successful business families—the *Journey Up* and the *Journey Across*—encompass developmental stages with predictable stressors. Families are strained by these massive shifts in culture, often to the point of breaking. What actually makes these two transitions so difficult is that they are unexpected and unexamined by the family itself.

In this book we will look at the common evolutions of culture within successful business families, impacted from forces both external and internal to the family. Families are affected by external influences as they interact with different cultures in the course of their business and economic development. More importantly, they encounter powerful internal pressures as family members in successive generations are shaped by cultures outside their parents' experience.

These cultural pressures typically build over years but, much like the tectonic tension preceding seismic events, appear manageable to those within the family. The point where pressure erupts often occurs during transitional periods such as succession in the family business or generational transitions in power or position. It is then that families are rocked by the upheavals that had been building from the cross-generational and cross-cultural strains within the family.

Families live these transitions but, like culture itself, do not have perspective on what they are going through. Culture tends to be invisible to those within it. Families sense they are undergoing significant change, but they often have little understanding of what is happening and no language to describe the process.

Fortunately, the transitions themselves do not have to be inherently damaging or inevitably destructive. We believe that, by exploring the cultural dimension, we can offer families and their advisors a path to productive negotiation of new solutions. By seeing their challenges as cultural rather than personal, families can become less defensive about maintaining their traditions in the face of natural and inevitable change. They can open up to new possibilities that selectively integrate values, behaviors, traditions, and policies of other cultures. As we will see, families can successfully adapt by embracing the blend of cultures inhabited by global family enterprises.

Notice the global themes, for example, in this fictionalized but increasingly common scenario involving two family enterprises:

A Global Family Begins Its Journeys: A Case Example (Part I of 4)[4]

Wen Ho and his wife Li-Peng were each raised in a farming village in mainland China around the mid-Twentieth Century. Joined in an arranged marriage, they were humble people raised with centuries-old traditions emphasizing the collective family with reverence for elders and ancestors. Their personalities were forged with values of respect for others and the preservation of harmonious relationships by limiting discussion of conflicts. They understood that their needs and desires were secondary to family, community, and government.

When the opportunity for private ownership of business arose in the early 1980s, Mr. Wen decided to open a small factory making clothing using local textiles. He began selling to American clothing companies seeking Chinese factories with inexpensive labor. He made many mistakes in entrepreneurship but learned quickly, becoming a man of respect and relative wealth in the region.

Wen Ho and Li-Peng were blessed with two intelligent and resourceful daughters, Wen Yan and Wen Li-Feng, raised with traditional Asian values including obedience and subservience. Sent to London for college education, the daughters soon became familiar with Western behaviors and attitudes alongside their Asian upbringing. Wen Yan began using the name Vanessa for British ears, while Wen Li-Feng called herself Lisa. As each learned to dress and speak differently, they also were exposed to ideas about greater gender equality, assertiveness, and self-sufficiency.

Saving their money carefully, Vanessa and Lisa would use short school vacations to make trips around France, Spain, Italy, and Greece. It was during one of these trips to Barcelona that Vanessa met Simón Borrego.

Simón was the eldest in a third-generation well-respected Spanish manufacturing family with roots going back to the 1920s. His father Juan ran the family enterprise as a benevolent but powerful patriarch. Juan kept information closely guarded within an inner circle composed predominantly of family members. Only in this way could the family insure that its secrets would remain safe from competitors and intrusive, ever-changing governments. It took a long time for outsiders to build trust and establish business relationships with the family, though once established, those business relationships were carefully maintained. Family relationships were sometimes volatile in the Latin tradition, with constant vigilance to commanding respect and defending reputation. Challenges to Juan's authority were allowed within the family only to a limited extent, with disagreements kept under the surface. But above all else, family was cherished.

As the oldest son in his own branch, Simón was groomed from an early age to eventually lead the family. As was expected, when the time came he went off to college and then business school in England, earning the high grades that were also expected. But the more he was exposed to his classes, the mentoring he received from experienced professors, and the lives of his classmates, the more he began to question his predetermined role in his family's business.

Part of the attraction between Vanessa Wen and Simón Borrego was their experiences of a close family running a family enterprise and its obligations. But they also were developing a sense of freedom to make choices based on a much broader world of options. Some of their choices could potentially put them at odds with their parents, not the least of which was choosing a life partner from a country and culture far outside their families' experience. There was also the future of the family enterprises to consider, the obligations of family, and the complex blending of cultures from Asia, Spain, and England.

How could this next generation work through important decisions, respecting their own needs and the needs of their families? How could their families understand the disruptions to tradition they themselves had set in motion? And, what techniques could they use to resolve the challenges they were facing?

To help families and the advisors who serve them, we describe the following elements through the course of this book:

- A grounding in the latest research about the core cultures around the world—the landscape upon which families make their journeys of wealth, enterprise, and success. We offer this as background to understand the nature of families in different cultures, no matter the economic level of the family.

- A short review of our concepts on how families make the economic *Journey Up* within whatever culture the family inhabits. This encompasses what we first described as the "Immigrants and Natives" metaphor, whereby some family members and generations make the migration to wealth from economic adversity while others are born into the environment of affluence.
- Fresh insights into the *Journey Across* whereby a family's success brings new ethnic cultural influences into the family system. We discuss how successful families naturally encounter a global culture that has strongly Western influences as well as other ethnic elements.
- Actionable recommendations for how families can understand and navigate these two transitions. We explain the use of negotiation strategies drawn from organizations and businesses who have staff from diverse cultures, adapted for use in family enterprises. We also discuss the role of advisors in helping families cope with cross-cultural conflicts.

The strains that some families endure in facing these journeys are profound. Some families do not survive the transitions. But those that do are able to do more than survive; they truly thrive. They adapt resiliently as they navigate cultural boundaries and interact with people holding assumptions quite different than their own. Their destiny moves far beyond their roots to the world at large.

SECTION I

The Three Global Cultures

CHAPTER 2

Surveying the Landscape: Understanding Culture

To explore any territory, a few tools are necessary. These are the compasses, the maps, the landmarks used to keep track of progress and identify the geography. Although there are many ways for families or advisors to understand what differentiates cultures, a few elements have been found to be most useful.

Core Elements of Cultural Systems

Traditionally, researchers have relied on differentiating cultures through specific features or scales along various dimensions. A pioneering model developed by Edwin T. Hall[5] defined *high context* and *low context* cultures. This referred to the degree to which cultures embed verbal communication within a broader framework of cues and situation (high-context communication) compared to cultures that rely on the message alone to explain itself (low-context communication).

A high-context culture, as in Asia for example, leaves many aspects of a message unstated. This process assumes that people share a history and understanding that allows them to grasp the full meaning of the message. They can use fewer words because people "read between the lines" to understand a message. In Korea, this ability is called *nunchi*, roughly translated as "measuring with eyes…. The person who possesses *nunchi* is good at reading the feelings and state of mind of others by observing their nonverbal messages."[6]

In contrast, low-context cultures use words more extensively to specify explicitly what is meant. They are less attuned to subtle messages and social cues, which may cause them to miss the deeper meaning of an exchange or interaction. In the West, communication experts actively discourage couples or organizational team members from "engaging in mind-reading" as too risky, indirect, and unassertive. "Be direct!" is the mantra.

Low-context, explicit individuals will appear to be very literal-minded to colleagues adept with ambiguity. Individuals from cultures comfortable with ambiguous high-context communication may find themselves misunderstood in low-context cultures. High-context communicators may also find themselves uncomfortable when asked to make things more explicit.

Saying No without Saying No

In an advisor training workshop, participants formed into groups of three to practice communication skills. They focused on learning to give empathic responses to personal self-disclosures of the client in simulated role-playing scenarios. The North American-based advisors engaged in reasonable self-disclosure when playing the client or the advisor in the practices.

When the time came for one female Asian participant to play the role of the client, she had little to say. Pressed by her role-play partner to find some emotional issue he could delve into, she cast her eyes down and said, "I'm sorry, I don't have a particularly interesting life." Her fellow participants assumed she was either anxious, shy, or had low self-esteem.

Only upon later discussion did this participant reveal she found the emotional self-disclosure of the exercise to be horrifyingly personal in front of strangers. Yet, for her to say so directly would be overly assertive. In her mind, she risked bringing embarrassment to the workshop leader and the other participants if she objected to the exercise. Taking the blame by being "uninteresting" was meant to be understood as a diplomatic way to dodge sharing information before trust had been built. Unfortunately, she was using a high-context, indirect communication technique no one could read.

This cultural dimension alone is highly relevant in advising to family enterprises. A low-context Western consultant trying to define every aspect of a family agreement may find it frustrating to work with an

Asian or Middle Eastern family comfortable with a great deal of ambiguity, including a willingness to craft agreements that stress general principles rather than making explicit rules and policies.

OTHER KEY FACTORS

Geert Hofstede[7] developed a model based on the behavioral tendencies of members of a culture along multiple dimensions, allowing comparison across cultures. One key dimension encompassed *individualism versus collectivism*, referring to the degree to which an individual is integrated with and identifies with a group (a family, a company, or even a country). An individualist orientation stresses personal achievements and individual rights, while a collective orientation embeds personal identity within long-term commitments to a group. Hofstede analyzed other dimensions such as *power distance* (the degree to which power is concentrated in a few people versus distributed to many group members with more cooperative relationships), *tolerance versus intolerance for uncertainty*, *long-term versus short-term orientation*, and *self-indulgence versus restraint*. Fons Trompenaars and Charles Hampden-Turner have added elegant expansions of these and other factors, with insightful work recently on related dimensions by Erin Meyer of the international business school INSEAD.[8]

Six Dimensions Differentiating Cultures

Drawing from various cross-cultural models, six core dimensions may be most relevant to global family enterprises:

1. The Primary Unit of the Culture:
   The Individual or the Collective Family?

What is the fundamental element of a culture? Some cultures see the larger *whole* or *collective system* — the nation, organization, or the family — as most important. Individuals must find their place and form their identity within this larger unit. Other cultures focus on the *individual*, the autonomous person who can accept or decline to participate in larger systems and whose independent choices are most important.

    Major rights and obligations are linked to the fundamental cultural unit. In collective systems, the group or tribe has primacy. The individual is subservient to the family or the tribe and must adhere to his or her role within it. In individualistic systems, the individual is primary. The family, tribe, or organization is meant to serve individual interests.

These two types of systems have also been described as having qualities of being *tight* or *loose*.[9] In tight cultures the social structure is highly defined and controls options, whereas in loose cultures, individuals are less closely associated or controlled, sometimes with multiple allegiances to several different groups or communities.

As we shall see, the individual-collective dimension is highly relevant for family enterprises as generations unfold. Whether the family is tightly organized as a pre-eminent system or is loosely-affiliated as a group of individuals opting to work together becomes especially important in the second or third generation of a family enterprise. That is when family members — making the *Journey Up* from modest economic circumstances to wealth — determine how interconnected they want to be. Do they embrace the interdependence of wealth or split into independent family branches going their own way? It is also when second- or third-generation members, making the *Journey Across* to other ethnic cultures, begin to realize there is a world of independence and self-determination outside the family system. How the family achieves its balance of independence and interdependence is one of its major challenges in adapting to wealth and success.

2. The Nature of Power and Decision-making: Hierarchical or Consensus-driven?

Decisions can either flow hierarchically from the family leader down or be based on democratic, shared thinking. Do power and authority lie with a single leader at the top, or are these dispersed collaboratively within the group? To what degree are members free to make decisions in their areas of expertise or responsibility? If decision-making is based on lines of authority, then obedience and commitment are owed to any decision made via the proper channels.

Two related qualities follow from this dimension of power and authority. One quality is how close to or far from power other family members feel, in relation to the leader (the *power distance* described earlier). This influences family members' sense of participation in the decisions affecting their own life. For those who prefer autonomy over dependency, it can make the difference between staying with or leaving the family.

The other quality influences how conflict and communication are handled when differences arise. Can family members express differences or must they keep silent in order to show respect and avoid disharmony?

3. The Nature of Communication: Ambiguous or Specific?

Communication styles can vary greatly across cultures, impacting the degree to which messages get sent clearly and received accurately. This dimension, cited at the beginning of this chapter, refers to whether communication is highly contextual (ambiguous, inferential, and mindful of any potential impacts on relationship and face-saving) or relies largely on the specific words being spoken (direct, assertive, and specific). "Say what you mean, mean what you say" lies at one end of this dimension, while adept mind-reading and inference lie at the other.

Communication style may come into play around the family council table, for example, when documents, policies or procedures are being crafted. One family may wish to specify agreements across generations using clear, precise language, while another family may be comfortable implying things using general principles and conditions. The family business consultant must understand the cultural context for communication and not see everything through his or her own cultural lens of communication.

4. Emotional Expression: Direct or Indirect?

Within relationships, how honest and open are people in expressing how they feel about each other and what is happening around them? Are emotions and issues handled openly and directly, with tolerance of any resulting conflict? Or, are feelings filtered, referenced obliquely, and possibly suppressed in favor of keeping the peace? This factor captures how much people are able to contemplate sharing their ideas and feelings, especially in situations where they feel they should (or are expected to) defer to authorities, especially within the family. Communication about ideas or topics may be permitted; emotional expression may not be. Alternatives in various cultures may include using third parties to intercede about personal matters or using subtle or indirect pressure tactics to induce change.

This dimension is relevant for predicting how well families may cope with the natural emotional stress occurring during personal or family transitions, such as in discussing succession, careers, leadership, or marriage. Many a family has encountered impasses in normal generational dilemmas simply because they could not approach the issues in effective ways.

This is not to say that directness is the only effective means of addressing problems; advocating directness is a Western cultural bias. But whatever style of emotional expression is used must be effective in surfacing relevant issues, dealing with alternative views, and negotiating a workable solution within cultural norms of power, authority, and collaboration.

5. Establishing Trust: Task-based or Relationship-based?

Trust between individuals or groups may be assumed and granted based on various methods. It can be based on the nature of the relationship and broad affiliations with other trusted or powerful groups (a *relationship* basis) or derived from the outcome of specific actions and interactions with the person at hand (a *task* basis). Whether trust is grounded in specific tasks with individuals in the present situation or in broad networks, relationships, and institutions varies by culture. Task-based cultures focus more on what you do, while relationship cultures focus more on whom you are and whom you know.

In a task-based environment, individuals build trust with people they interact with based on an accumulating set of experiences that determine whether someone seems reliable and worthy of trust. They also assume the other person will speak up and let others know what the individual wants and needs in a direct, assertive manner. Here, trust is individual to the person, and each person must stand or fall on their own trustworthiness. Two people working side by side in Western culture, for example, may come to trust each other as they show up on time, work diligently, resolve problems together, and support each other's efforts. They may not know each other's personal lives very much, but they do know they can trust each other when they work together.

By contrast, in a relationship-based culture, people trust others based upon the affiliations they have and/or the extended personal relationships they build as they get to know each other. They do not trust those they do not know well, and they may initially mistrust those not within their relationship circle. Two people working side by side in Middle-Eastern or Latin American cultures, for example, may be formal and wary of each other until they discover they come from extended families with a longstanding history of good relations. They may spend time sharing meals, describing their family relationships, and attending celebrations with each other's families such as birthdays and weddings.

How trust is built, maintained, damaged and repaired is very relevant when misunderstandings arise in generational family enterprises. The choices people make, how they fulfill a sense of trust, and the relative primacy of the individual or the family all come into play in generating feelings of loyalty or betrayal in the eyes of one family branch or generation with another.

Elder generations relying on a relationship basis for trust may prefer that younger generations find marital partners within known groups or affiliations. They may also be wary of outsiders coming into the family. In contrast, second- or third-generation family members, educated and working in the West with its task-basis for trust, may be perfectly comfortable attaching themselves to individuals they meet in the course of their careers as they build a history of trustworthy experiences.

6. Approach to Problem Solving: Analyze the Parts or Understand the Whole?

Problems that arise in families or organizations can be approached as individual standalone issues or embedded in a larger context. Analytical, rational thinking breaks things down into component parts and deals with specifics. Holistic, integrated, contextual thinking looks at the whole system and seeks solutions in context.

Some cultures attack problems "as they are." They look for causes and effects, seek solutions from a defined array of options, and evaluate the success of problem-solving by what follows directly in time and situation. Other cultures see problems as in an ecosystem, Challenges in one part of the system may have (or cause) ripple effects in other areas that must be accommodated when finding solutions. Preserving the integrity of the system may be paramount over fixing one small part—or person—having difficulty.

This dimension is relevant for how a family approaches the natural developmental problems that arise over the course of the family or its enterprise. Some family members may see issues as interconnected and in need of slow thoughtful discourse, while others raised in a different culture may tackle issues as discrete independent problems. A component-oriented family would feel comfortable implementing a particular service, product or transaction to address a wealth-planning issue, such as creating an estate plan largely to minimize taxes. A holistic view would first look at the wider goals and context of the family, asking whether this is the right thing to do at this time and how it will fit with other efforts.

Each approach has its merits. Families experience strain, however, when members comfortable with different problem-solving orientations advocate for particular strategies that seem foreign, unproductive, or inefficient to others. This is when words like "immature," "pig-headed," "stubborn," "old-fashioned," "impulsive" or "narrow-minded" begin flying around in family meetings.

Putting the Dimensions Together

The use of polarities or dimensions is a useful tool for understanding what culture means and how cultures differ. When families have always lived within a single cultural perspective, they will believe theirs is the only, or the only correct, way to behave. This works well until the outside world intrudes, often in the form of a family member who comes from or gets exposed to another culture. Then, the family is faced with differences that must be resolved.

We will now move on to a major new conceptual framework incorporating well-established dimensions of culture. This new paradigm is advancing the fields of cross-cultural psychology and organizational management. It also opens up important new frameworks for understanding the challenges of global family enterprises.

CHAPTER 3

The Three Global Cultures

Recent advances in cross-cultural psychology reveal that the elements mentioned in Chapter 2 coalesce into three distinct patterns of national and ethnic culture.[10] These three emerging clusters are highly relevant to understanding change within family enterprise. They explain what we ourselves have seen in working with families, and they provide a major step forward in conceptualizing both problems and solutions for global family enterprises.

The following three patterns have emerged:

Individualist culture: Western culture, including the United States, Canada, Great Britain, Northern Europe and Australia

Collective Harmony culture: East Asian culture, including China, Hong Kong, Singapore, Korea, and Japan

Honor culture: A diverse ethnic cluster consisting of Latin America, Southern and Eastern Europe, the Middle East, India, Russia, and Africa

In the cross-cultural literature, these three cultures are identified according to several core measures[11] but especially according to how individuals' self-worth is determined.[12] Western culture is termed *Dignity* culture in the literature because self-worth is largely determined internally by the individual, is highly focused on personal dignity, tends to be stable across time and situations, and is not easily disrupted by social influences. East Asian culture is labeled *Face* culture since self-worth is largely externally derived and reinforced by social influences in reciprocal ways. *Honor* cultures forge self-worth based on reputation and social respect; one's sense of honor and position is forged partly by oneself and partly by the hierarchies one inhabits. We offer a more natural-language nomenclature for family businesses and their advisors,

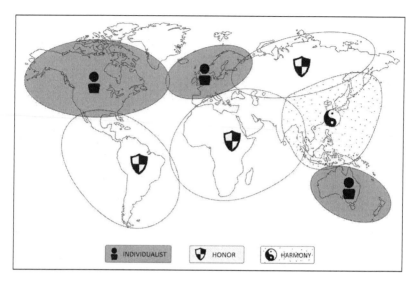

Figure 3-1: Map of the three major ethnic cultures

suggesting the terms *Individualist* (Dignity), *Collective Harmony* (Face), and *Honor* cultures.

The three cultures have arisen in different parts of the world at different times. *Honor* culture is the oldest and most universal, persisting to varying degrees today in Southern and Eastern Europe, the Middle East, India, Russia, Latin America, South Asia and Africa. *Collective Harmony* developed in East Asia from Confucian and other Eastern religions and traditions. The most recently developed form is the rational *Individualist* culture, arising in Great Britain and Northern Europe and spreading in a colonial pattern to North America and Australia. Individualist culture is now influencing many areas around the world.

Each tradition incorporates cultural patterns that influence the expectations, practices, and behavior of family enterprises in those regions. In a global interconnected world, however, these cultural styles are no longer strictly tied to places. As individuals migrate from one culture to another, they retain cultural values and attitudes from their heritage as they adopt new modes of interacting. Israel, for example, contains many immigrant groups that blend Individualist and Honor cultures. India and North Africa, whose educational and political systems developed according to British Colonial models, also incorporate elements of the Individual model within their Honor roots. Japan has strong Harmony qualities but exhibits certain Individualist traits that influence its business dealings and negotiation strategies. Indonesia incorporates multiple elements drawn from Muslim cultures, Asian influences, and even some Western Individualist features.

A country as diverse as the United States contains sub-cultures that reflect different styles. While the US is clearly an Individualist culture, southern states share many features consistent with the Honor style as a result of their multicultural influences.

Europe has many variations. To the north, Scandinavian and Anglo-Saxon nations stress the rule of law and respect for individuals, taking an analytical approach to problem-solving in the Individualist tradition. Southern Europe (e.g., Italy, Greece, Spain) tends toward abstract notions of right and wrong, holistic problem-solving, and the importance of one's place in the family, placing it more in the Honor frame. Cultural differences also reflect personal style and communication; Southern European countries tend to be more expressive, direct and emotional while the North is more rational, inhibited and explicitly rules-based.

High-Stress Negotiations between Very Dissimilar Cultures

The impact of differing perspectives on negotiations could be seen in the contentious, highly controversial process of creating the 2015 agreement between the United States and Iran over Iran's nuclear capabilities. Issues aside, achieving an agreement between these two countries was difficult in part because of communication and cognitive styles. The low-context/low ambiguity/task-based-trust orientation of Western countries focused on defining details and specific actions to be completed in order to prove compliance. Iranian negotiators focused on respect for their country, their sovereignty, and their national honor as the foundation for agreement, with greater tolerance for ambiguity about details. Any agreement had to reconcile these very opposing views of autonomy, trust, communication, and tolerance for uncertainty. Imagine if the negotiators represented different generations of a family—a traditional Middle-Eastern patriarch and his Western-educated children.

It pays to be cautious about immediately assuming certain personality traits just because someone comes from a particular culture. As Brett points out,

> [T]hese cultural styles are central tendencies that characterize large population groups as generalities. Individuals or families will demonstrate their own patterns of problem-solving, communication, family orientation, or trust building along a spectrum unique for each culture.[13]

Yet research does demonstrate that people share common orientations based on the culture of their heritage. Being mindful of culture can illuminate what at first blush appears to be simply individual personality. Each of the three cultural styles possesses a coherence and overall structure that helps to understand the operation of business families.

The Three Cultures along Multiple Dimensions

The three cultural styles would be expected to differ widely according to their tendencies along the six dimensions described in Chapter 2. Erin Meyer of INSEAD has used data compiled from cross-cultural negotiating and management situations to assess where different countries fit along these and other scales. Her excellent book, *The Culture Map: Breaking through the Invisible Boundaries of Global Business*, provides guidance to multiple dimensions related to communication, providing feedback, learning new information, leadership style, decision-making, trust building, conflict management, and time orientation.[14] Distilling her "culture maps" into the three global culture styles reveals a consistent pattern where Individualist culture lies toward one end of each scale, Collective Harmony lies at the other, and Honor culture takes an intermediate position, close to Collective Harmony culture in many respects (see Figure 3-2).

Some of these dimensions have already been explained, such as the nature of communication, leadership, decision-making, trust, and disagreement across cultures. Erin Meyer also describes cultural differences along other dimensions:

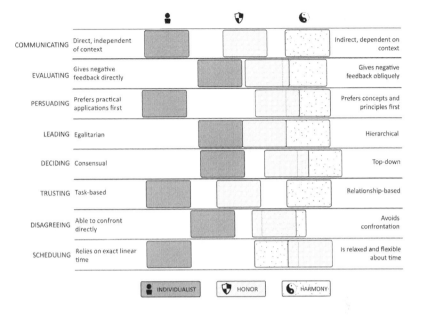

Figure 3-2: The three major global cultures along eight dimensions. Adapted from material originally presented in Erin Meyer, *The Culture Map*, 2014

- **Evaluating:** Some cultures handle the conveying of negative feedback by being direct to the point of bluntness. Others prefer to embed criticism within carefully crafted layers of positive comments or polite indirectness.
- **Persuading:** Some cultures prefer to hear and focus on the practical applications of proposed solutions first, followed by the theory or concepts behind those applications. Other cultures prefer to have the conceptual framework for a proposal explained first, building toward conclusions about how solutions may be implemented. In other words, some cultures like to hear the headline first, then the story. Others want the background carefully explained before getting to the bottom line.
- **Scheduling:** Some cultures are precise and linear in managing time, valuing promptness and good time management. Each planned appointment and event follows another in good order.

Others are highly flexible about being on time. They are more focused on enjoying activities and events without much regard to careful time management. As might be expected, members of one culture get easily exasperated with other cultures on this one dimension alone.

Building Cultural Intelligence

Using these dimensions and others more specific to family enterprises, the next three chapters go into detail about the Individualist, Collective Harmony, and Honor styles.

We offer these descriptions as a guide for families and advisors to understand common cultural attitudes, beliefs, and behaviors that otherwise might be thought of as individual personality or inclination. Adopting this perspective as a family requires openness and a particular type of emotional intelligence — cultural intelligence. Cultural intelligence is the ability to suspend one's own cultural perspectives and grasp the cultural patterns of people from other groups.[15] People with good cultural intelligence are able to consider their options before they act. Then, through negotiation and exchange, members of different cultures learn to collaborate in an environment that understands and accepts each perspective. In our emphasis on adaptation as a key driver of generational success, we view cultural intelligence as an increasingly useful competence for families and advisors.

Two Global Families Face Cross Cultural Stress
(Part 2 of 4)

After much discussion, Simón Borrego and Vanessa Wen decided to marry upon his graduation from business school. Both families were initially less than pleased. Vanessa's parents remained polite but asked probing questions about children and long-term plans. Simón's family had louder discussions, sometimes with threats and accusations. In the end, both families reluctantly blessed Simón and Vanessa's union.

The overarching question remained: Where would they live? Simón heard clearly his father's strong request that he return home to the business. But doubts had been brewing in Simón's mind since before he had met Vanessa. He felt constrained by the limits of the family business, believing there was a lack of opportunity for expansion and for the new ideas learned in business courses. Plus, he was concerned about having to wait a very long time under the control of his traditional father who would retain all the power. Having been exposed to fresh thinking in business school, he began to entertain the idea he might be happier and freer if he did not return to his family's enterprise.

Vanessa felt the equally strong expectation to return to her own family and its business. She also recognized she felt neither prepared for nor interested in a business career. Her sister Lisa had returned to Hong Kong (where the family now resided), married a young Singaporean attorney, and fit herself into the family traditions. When would Vanessa rejoin the family?

The answer to Vanessa and Simón's dilemma unfolded to everyone's surprise.

As Simón got to know Wen Ho, the two men developed a surprising bond. Simón was taken with the incredible possibilities he saw in China to grow the clothing business. With his European connections, his friends from his education, his MBA, and his background expertise in manufacturing, he sensed opportunities to become a major supplier of European clothing brands. He believed he could make a greater contribution to Wen Ho's business than to his own family's operations. He also liked that he would be the only male working in the next generation of the Asian family business and would not have to navigate the more-traditional views of his Spanish cousins and his brother.

Despite his affection and respect for Simón Borrego, Wen Ho had his own concerns to consider. He had a Chinese business to think of; it was a mixed blessing to have a Western family member in management there. Simón also had much to learn about Asian culture. These included how to maintain his "face" honorably as well as others', and how to contain his feeling and his opinions, revealing only well-controlled morsels at chosen times. But times were changing, and fortunately, many of Simón's Spanish traditions were in line with Wen Ho's:

- How to build trusted relationships with business partners slowly, after many meals and social interactions.
- How to keep private information closely guarded.

- How to be a firm yet wise leader in his own home.

Simón informed his family he was going to try working with Wen Ho. As expected, the Borrego family was very upset. Simon's father felt deeply betrayed by his son's choice. Juan saw this as dishonoring the family and damaging the reputation of the business. Yet behind the scenes, his cousins and his brother were more than delighted at the sudden vacuum in family leadership. Educated in the US and Spain but more aligned with the patriarch, they quietly saw opportunities of their own to expand the family enterprise in new directions.

Simón and Vanessa embarked on their flight back to Hong Kong to start the next phase of their own lives and each of their family enterprises.

Acknowledging Differences within Generalities

We reiterate that these styles define central tendencies in large groups around certain types of behavior. Many nations have different ethnic groups and traditions that operate slightly differently. While these models describe modal tendencies, the actual behavior of individuals or groups is distributed along a bell curve. Individuals and families may exhibit higher or lower levels of each element.

These models also articulate general orientations of the family enterprises that emerge from each of these cultural traditions. Not all families will demonstrate all of the characteristics to the same degree. In addition, as cultures interact, they borrow qualities that enable them to operate more effectively, further diluting the cultural specificity of these tendencies. With increasing geographic mobility, families move from one traditional culture to another, blending cultural styles rather than maintaining pure traditions. Just as people are unique within broad general characteristics, so are families.

Let us now examine the general characteristics of cultures around the globe.

CHAPTER 4

Individualist Culture

Northern Europe, the United Kingdom, North America and Australia share a cultural style steeped in principles of individualism, where the purpose of larger institutions is to support the independence and self-worth of each individual. The family's purpose is to help each individual member develop a fulfilling life, maximizing his or her potential. Rather than members of a family or organization being subordinate to the whole, the whole is subordinate to each individual's willing participation.

The Rise of the Individual

Individualist culture is about meritocracy, accountability, personal achievement, rationality and visible success providing results. These values arose with the Protestant Reformation in Europe and were further refined through the ideals of representative democracy and capitalism. The French and American revolutions, with their ethic of personal entrepreneurship and their rejection of dynastic titles and privileges, challenged the European tradition of hereditary inheritance of wealth and social status. While wealth-creating patriarchs (and, increasingly, matriarchs) certainly have earned privileges, those privileges are limited in scope and time.

During the Reformation, religious elders' traditional authority over access to the Divine was replaced by an evangelical tradition where everyone now had a direct line to God. Beliefs became personal; each individual could be his own authority. More recently, the Sixties elevated the emphasis on personal identity and self-actualization. Within the family, parents could have their authority challenged (even business founders!). Personal obligation to the family was diminished, although the expectation of wealth transfers from parents may not have diminished to quite the same extent.

As T. M. Luhrman, a Stanford University professor of religion, notes:

> Americans and Europeans stand out from the rest of the world for our sense of ourselves as individuals. We like to think of ourselves as unique, autonomous, self-motivated, self-made. As the anthropologist Clifford Geertz observed, this is a peculiar idea. People in the rest of the world are more likely to understand themselves as interwoven with other people — as interdependent, not independent. In such social worlds, your goal is to fit in and adjust yourself to others, not to stand out. People imagine themselves as part of a larger whole — threads in a web, not lone horsemen on the frontier. In America, we say that the squeaky wheel gets the grease. In Japan, people say that the nail that stands up gets hammered down.[16]

In Individualist culture, the self develops internally and stabilizes over time; self-worth comes from within. The concept of self-esteem is an inherently individualistic notion, developed by finding and pursuing one's personal passions. Children are praised for their individual achievements and expected to seek their own path in life.

The influential therapist Murray Bowen's family systems theory identifies certain imperatives assumed to be universal across cultures. These include *individuation* of each young family member and the development of the capacity to evaluate and resist group pressures based on one's personal views. In a family systems perspective, the formation of one's individual identity, separate from the family's identity and functioning, is a necessary stage of adult development. As mentioned in Chapter 1, this is a Western perspective that elevates individualism as the ultimate goal of personal development, ignoring other ways to blend and balance the individual and the family.

Individualist Culture: Crisis in a Middle American Manufacturing Family[17]

A Midwestern American food manufacturing company arose over two generations out of one family's farming activities and the development of an innovative product. The family expanded to similar products into the third generation, with many family members enjoying employment in the business under a charismatic family leader. The family shared many core values and a religious tradition of service to the community.

During the third generation, the enterprise experienced a crisis. While the business was growing, profits were diminishing. Members from various branches of the family had different levels of ownership, spread amongst nearly fifty people. The business was plagued by rivalries and conflict in the second and third generations, which led to disagreements over policies, distribution of dividends and profits, and who was to hold major roles.

The emerging fourth generation (G4) became concerned and began to meet as a group. They discussed openly the conflicts they observed among the second-generation siblings, including some in-laws who felt that what they were receiving in financial distributions was inadequate relative to the size of the business. More importantly, an impending struggle over leadership grew within the enterprise.

The G4s felt change was necessary at many levels. With their Individualist orientation, they viewed questioning the family's leadership as a rational and prudent response to the problems in the enterprise. They began a review of the business and the performance of family leaders. Considerable turmoil resulted when a key family leader was asked to leave his position, even though his branch was a major shareholder. Although all family members were still invited to enter the business, G4 wanted to insure that those who worked for the enterprise were accountable for results. They also developed and supported the work of non-family executives for key leadership positions. Still, the family experienced significant anxiety as the breakdown in leadership, insistent voices of the younger generation, and insecurity of the family enterprise all escalated at once.

Upon reaching maturity in Individualist culture, family members are able to withstand challenges to their self-esteem and independence because they have a secure inner sense of who they are. Some aspects of the self are socially determined—nationality, race, economic level, religious affiliation. Yet there is tremendous freedom to establish one's personal identity within these larger group identities, including the freedom to change affiliations when desired. People can change religious or political affiliations as easily as they change clothing.

EGALITARIANISM, TRUST, AND LEADERSHIP

The Individualist cultural style holds the aspirational value that everyone has equal rights and responsibilities. There is less emphasis on social or authoritarian hierarchies compared to other cultures. Leaders are elected democratically from a wide range of social classes. Within the family, generational status and, to a certain extent, birth order may convey authority, but by adulthood these patterns weaken. Men and women are assumed to be equal. The egalitarian ethos is visible in the extreme informality of the United States, where people eschew titles and quickly engage in using first names on a friendly basis.

People assume or develop trust with others based on who they are as individuals and the tasks people share, not linked to clan relationships or levels of authority. Let someone down, though, and trust may be damaged enough to be irreparable.

In business and decision-making, the tradition of a strong single authoritarian leader has been supplanted by the model of leaders working with a strong team of competitive and committed peers. The legitimacy of the leader must be earned via the trust of his followers or else risk removal.

Although authority may be less hierarchical than in the other two cultures, individualism still reigns with decisive leaders. This is certainly true in many family enterprises. Especially in American business culture, the stress on individualism and entrepreneurship means that businesses are typically built by single visionary leaders. Edgar Schein, who developed many of the founding principles defining corporate culture, notes that in the past fifty years there has been little genuine support for team functioning, even as the concept of the team has been given lip-service.[18] He observes that, even in teams, the emphasis is on individual heroes and achievements more than those of the whole group. Whether this is finally giving way in the Millennial generation to a more socially-distributed, truly collaborative approach may be intriguing to consider.

A prominent feature of Individualist culture is that the leader's authority is tempered by the overriding rule of law. Rule-based governance guides decision-making, insures fair dealings, and counters overzealous attempts by any one individual to grab power. Individualist nations tend to have relatively stable governments, a benefit which allows their citizens to trust the rule of law and pursue their individual goals freely. Individualist nations also tend to have a well-developed legal system to help settle disputes about competing rights.

In Individualist culture, the assumption is that decisions will be made based on linear cause-and-effect analysis of component problems. Tradition is not a reason to continue; "what works" is more important than "we've always done it this way." Decisions are to be supported by data and arrived at by open rational discussion. Fairness is important in this model. When a family or organization is fair, everyone's interests are taken into account through a process of open expression of differences.

DIRECT, OPEN COMMUNICATION

In general, communication and expression are direct, assertive, revealing of emotions and self-disclosing, yet subordinated to logic and rationality. Individualist subcultures certainly vary in their norms on self-disclosure (compare Americans with the British, or the Swedes) yet as a broad culture the Individualist style is generally more encouraging of self-expression than the Collective Harmony or Honor cultures. Business communications are supposed to be rational and non-emotional, but within families and relationships there is great tolerance for the open expression of feelings, thoughts, and ideas.

The concepts of obligation, duty, service, and loyalty to family are present but not prominent in Individualist culture. These concepts tend to be associated mostly with military- or paramilitary-type organizations or clubs that have a strong ethic of member loyalty. If anything, the highly democratic emphasis is on transparency, sharing of ideas, and the valuing of innovative ideas from younger generations. As a result, the voices of next-generation family members can be heard and heeded. They see legitimacy in questioning their elders rather than dutifully accepting guidance. Other cultures view this as insolent, selfish and even a bit narcissistic. It seems too "me-oriented," lacking any sense of the collective "we."

Along the *loose* versus *tight* societal dimension, Individualistic cultures are more loosely connected than the Honor and Harmony cultures. With individuals basing their life decisions less and less on previous tradition or the will of others, traditional institutions such as marriage have undergone transformations. Cherishing freedom and flexibility over commitment, young Individualists have been increasingly postponing or declining marriage in favor of cohabitation.[19] They feel freer to end relationships which don't seem to be working.

INDIVIDUALISM AND GLOBAL BUSINESS

More so than in the other two cultural styles, Individualist principles of rationality, specificity, explicit rules and expectations, performance and accountability are associated with the rise of global business. Individualist perspectives are represented in the culture of many public companies due to the regulation and compliance requirements of global markets. The Individualist style, stressing rationality and achievement, may be more agile and adaptable than cultures based on tradition, loyalty, and obligation. Enterprises in Harmony and Honor cultures face challenges from this perspective as they advance in business.

Individualist Culture: Resolving a Crisis in a Middle American Manufacturing Family

In the business family described above, the extended family began to develop its governance under G4's leadership, with an emphasis on fostering each successive generation. G4 instituted the following in a manner highly consistent with Individualist culture:

- They created a family council with one elected representative from each family branch, meeting quarterly. The goals were to sustain the strength of the core business and to keep the family connected while individual branches and members pursued different paths. They made decisions as much as possible by consensus.

- They created programs and educational activities for the fourth and fifth generations.

- They affirmed that, although the business remained a special opportunity for family members, each family member could also set his or her own sights elsewhere. They developed an extensive mentorship program to help young family members establish careers inside or outside the family enterprise.

- They created a "family bank" that would make loans to family members starting new businesses, with policies on accountability.
- They attended to areas where the family intersected with the business, such as setting dividend and employment policies.
- They held annual all-family gatherings to pursue recreational events, discuss common issues, and disseminate information transparently.
- They established a family office to oversee financial and some non-financial affairs for efficiencies of scale. They also began overseeing the philanthropic efforts within the family.

As a result of in-depth discussion and shared decision-making, a non-family executive was appointed to manage the business. Beyond the near-term decision, the family was not sure if the next enterprise leader would be a family executive or not. The family began to see themselves as owners more than operators of the business.

CHALLENGES OF INDIVIDUALISM

Despite its many strengths and growing dominance around the world, Individualist culture has significant drawbacks that can impact family enterprises. The major challenges for the Individualistic culture tend to be precisely the strengths of the other culture styles.

The emphasis on the individual over the family tribe can engender mistrust, competition, and difficulty working together. This is a challenge for business families trying to foster cooperation, interdependence and trust in their younger generations. By embracing youth, innovation, and new ideas so quickly, Individualist culture risks devaluing tradition, loyalty, and established wisdom.

Pursuing individual self-interest means that the authority and wisdom of tradition, elders, and the family may be under-appreciated. Individuals are less willing to compromise for collective goals, so that long-term objectives and the needs of the whole family can be overlooked. A further implication is that the family "glue" — the call to remain united as a family — may be thin. Each family member feels free to choose whether being part of the family enterprise is in their own self-interest. A common challenge is how to allow exit or autonomy from the family while still preserving strong family cohesion.

The rationality and lack of holistic contextual thinking also can lead issues to be posed as simplistic either/or choices rather than as more complex solutions having nuance and context. Finally, as we shall see in the journeys of the family across generations, the crucial aspect of interdependence may be ignored or discounted altogether, to the detriment of the family and its prosperity.

MOVING ON IN THE CULTURAL LANDSCAPE

Individualist culture occupies such a central position in the global landscape that other cultures seem to get less attention. But two other cultural styles have longer, deeper traditions and widespread influence. The next chapter brings forward East Asia, with its own advantages and challenges for families in business.

CHAPTER 5

Collective Harmony Culture

A second major cultural style is centered in the East Asia region, encompassing such countries as China, Hong Kong, Singapore, Korea, and (in certain aspects) Japan. These cultures are premised on Confucian principles elevating loyalty and obligation to family, respect for parents and other authorities, knowing one's place, and supporting the whole group rather than one's individual position.

Political scientist Robert Kaplan notes this tradition is rooted in the concepts of virtue and humaneness as well as the wisdom derived from a collective past.[20] This social system evolved over three millennia of remembered tradition. Collective Harmony culture prescribes behavior that fosters the culture as a whole. Consequently, it strongly influences family enterprises in this region:

> Confucianism is an ethical and philosophical system, emphasizing that human beings are teachable, improvable, and perfectible through personal and communal endeavor, especially self-cultivation. Confucianism also teaches the importance of observing one's role in relation to others, and the need to be obedient to authority. Its emphasis on morality, benevolence, and authority forms the foundation of paternalistic leadership... found to be prevalent among Chinese family firms operating in Taiwan and Southeast Asia.[21]

THE CENTRAL ROLE OF FACE IN SELF-WORTH

The concept of "face" is central to Collective Harmony culture, as it is in certain ways to Honor culture (but not to Individualist culture, a crucial distinction). The term has no exact counterpart in Western language. It contains elements of prestige, honor, respect, reputation and influence. However, it is much more socially-derived and -connected than the Individualist-focused equivalents of self-worth, shame, embarrassment, or social position:

> [Face] is something that is emotionally invested, and that can be lost, maintained, or enhanced, and must be constantly attended to in interaction. In general, people cooperate (and assume each other's cooperation) in maintaining face in interaction, such cooperation being based on the mutual vulnerability of face.[22]

In Individualist culture, each person is responsible for developing, maintaining, advocating for, and repairing his own self-esteem and self-respect. In Collective Harmony, the web of social relationships is much more influential in maintaining individuals' esteem. This is important because direct assertive communication may tear all too easily at the bonds between individuals and their social network if not handled carefully, especially in families.

TRADITION, FAMILY, OBLIGATION

In Collective Harmony culture, individuals respect the long heritage that has developed rules of order and harmony, rules which are not to be challenged lightly. A deep, often unspoken question is: "Who are you to challenge the wisdom built up over uncounted generations?" The first question asked of any new proposal is, "What does this mean for everyone, for the whole — the country, the community, the company, the family?" This view sees people as interwoven, interconnected, and part of a greater collective or clan.

Unlike Individualist culture where the self is internally generated, identity in Harmony culture is defined substantially by family, social interaction, and role. One's task in life is to honor one's family and live one's assigned role. As a result, change is slow. It proceeds only as the family as a whole becomes united around new directions together, rather than from individual initiative. Each son and daughter has an obligation to protect and nurture the family as well as to respect the long history of wisdom carried by traditions. Younger generations are expected to bring distinction to the family and not besmirch the reputation of the family or the enterprise.

Dishonor—Individual Fault or a Collective Stain?[23]

The differences between Individualism and Collective Harmony were well-defined in the "nut rage" incident involving Heather Cho (Korean name: Cho Hyun-ah) in 2014. Ms. Cho is the daughter of Korean Air chairman and CEO Cho Yang-ho, leader of this prominent regional enterprise. She reportedly became enraged with the cabin crew who served her macadamia nuts still in their packaging rather than on a plate as she expected. She assaulted one crew member, berated others, and commanded the plane to return to the gate, delaying the flight by twenty minutes.

When the incident became public, outrage followed. As would occur in the West, Ms. Cho was reprimanded severely, resigned, and suffered criminal charges with a subsequent prison sentence. Unlike in the West, however, Ms. Cho was not simply labelled as an entitled, self-centered executive who had exceeded her position. Her actions were seen in Korea as a reflection upon her family, the company, and the entire system of privilege enjoyed by large conglomerates (chaebols) over decades. Debate ensured as to whether the system should be changed so that the power of chaebols would be diminished. Her outrageous behavior over how she was served was widely seen as a systemic issue, much more so than would be the case in Individualist culture.

In Collective Harmony culture, elders are venerated. The authority of the patriarch derives from his place in the hierarchy and from acting in a wise, benevolent manner on behalf of the family. But loyalty owed to the patriarch is neither blind nor unlimited. There is a heavy responsibility for the patriarch to act nobly and wisely.

Women have a respected place and defined role, as do young people who are expected to be patient and wait their turn for roles holding responsibility. Relationships within the family are highly valued, and anything that disrupts or threatens relationships is to be avoided. This can entail costs to the family enterprise.

Patriarchal Authority Leading to Passivity

Two brothers owned a large Malaysian business, each with an eldest son working in the company. The uncles had limited education and managed the business over many years as they always had, not concerned with innovation. They were very dictatorial, expecting their offspring to just do what they were told and continue running the business as it always had been run.

The younger generation was frustrated. They felt their ideas were neither listened to nor taken seriously, and that they were not drawing on the elite business education they had received. They were not allowed to innovate or modernize the business, and they saw challenges ahead not being addressed.

Over time, the sons first thought of challenging their fathers more aggressively. After rejecting that, they entertained the idea of leaving the business. Eventually they each sank into a level of passive acceptance, waiting over years to inherit ownership and control. As they had forecast, the business began to decline, with profits and income down each year. The next generation felt they were out of options.

The pressure of obligation and loyalty within the family is high. It affects how members of the younger generation see their personal roles, especially the willingness to take on responsibilities within the family business. When called to work for the family business, next-generation members in Collective Harmony culture would instantly let go of what they are doing in order to respond. They would not think about their own compensation, ownership responsibilities, or status; they would fulfill their obligation. If they are hesitant about coming to work in the family, they would swallow any such reservations and expect to be treated fairly by their elders. Their Western counterparts would feel freer to raise more questions before considering this request.

Family and the Self across Cultures

The Joy Luck Club by Amy Tan provides a unique window into the contrasts between the Individualist style of America and the Collective Harmony style of Asian countries. These words about an American-born daughter, written by a Chinese mother who immigrated to the US, articulate the changing perspectives as the old modes of thinking give way to the new:

"I taught her how her American circumstances work. If you are born poor here, it's no lasting shame. You are the first in line for a scholarship. If the roof crashes on your head, no need to cry over this bad luck. You can sue anybody, make the landlord fix it. You do not have to sit like a Buddha under a tree letting pigeons drop their dirty business on your head. You can buy an umbrella. Or go inside a Catholic church. In America, nobody says you have to keep the circumstances somebody else gives you.

...but I couldn't teach her about Chinese character. How to obey parents and listen to your mother's mind. How not to show your own thoughts, to put your feelings behind your face so you can take advantage of hidden opportunities. Why easy things are not worth pursuing. How to know your own worth and polish it, never flashing it around like a cheap ring.

Don't be so old-fashioned, Ma. She told me... I'm my own person. And I think, How can she be her own person? When did I give her up?"[24]

INDIRECT, CONTEXTUAL COMMUNICATION AND BEHAVIOR

Communication and behavior in Collective Harmony culture are both oriented to sustaining relationships and mutual respect within social roles. A sign of respect is the willingness to not spell out issues or concerns directly. Indirect communication and ambiguity allow everyone to feel comfortable.

The language of Confucian culture is ambiguous, much more so than in Western languages. People in Collective Harmony culture are adept at understanding ambiguity and do not necessarily expect or want specifics to be spelled out. The meaning, the referent, and the tense of a phrase depend on their context. One simple example arose in the US about whether the pictogram character for the traditional Chinese year in 2015 represented a goat, a ram or a sheep. Speaking about this desire for more specificity, Chinese professor of folklore Zhao Shu summed up the implications of Eastern ambiguity:

> In Western culture, things are subdivided into more and more detailed categories, and that's why Europe has still not been unified after so many years... If you want to say whether it's goat or sheep, then why not ask whether it's a ewe or a ram? But Chinese culture has an inclusive spirit and stresses harmony.[25]

Decision-making and problem-solving are, like communication, contextual rather than explicit and analytical. Ambiguity creates flexibility for individual interpretation and response. However, this also leads to solo decision-making at the top, with a lack of transparency and lack of desire for input from others. Others' feelings or ideas are frequently to be kept hidden or suppressed for fear of offending the leader. Questions or objections easily can be interpreted as implying decisions are not wise or fully thought-through. If differences of opinion do arise, tactics and strategies by subordinates are more likely to remain hidden and implemented through long-term maneuvering rather than voiced openly in a productive (but potentially disharmonious) process of collaboration.

LEADERSHIP AND COLLECTIVE HARMONY

Leadership in Collective Harmony culture tends to be of the strong, solo type. On the surface, it appears much like the strong patriarchal leadership style familiar in Individualist culture. Leaders take counsel from advisors but ultimately exert authority based on their own decision-making. One leader we are familiar with noted that his decisions were meant to gain approval from his ancestors, not his children.

When leadership transition looms, the overwhelmingly dominant choice is how to replicate the strong solo governance model into the next generation. Either the eldest son will get the nod (whether capable or not) or another child will take the reins on behalf of his branch or the entire clan. To minimize conflicts, branches may each be given inherited assets under their own branch leadership and allowed to function somewhat separately.

Japan has had its own particular kinship tradition termed *ie* (pronounced *EE-ay*) with patriarchal leadership and a multigenerational family household. This tradition has held the lineage and rituals of the family and supported all family members. It is fading from modern Japanese life but has strong roots in Japanese culture.[26]

The concepts of shared leadership, collaboration, or the use of family councils for governance purposes are ironically foreign ideas in this collective-oriented culture. The family around the table may be tightly bound, but its Confucian-inspired leadership rests on a single pair of shoulders.

Allowing Individuals to Innovate within the Clan

Two brothers and their younger sister formed the third generation of a traditional Southeast Asian food-growing and production business. The enterprise prospered under the combined management of the eldest son and his brother, with their sister holding a small ownership share in addition to the support of her husband who worked in his own family business.

Each sibling had several children. The expectation was that the children of the brothers would go into the business. There was a possible place in the family enterprise for the sister's children as well, but no one discussed this very much. The elder generation expected the family to speak and act with one voice. The older brother, in contrast with his younger brother, was very conservative in his management of the business.

The family sent the young members of the fourth generation away for education in prominent Western business schools. As the G4s returned home with expectations of joining the business (including the sister's children), they began to think about starting new ventures. As might be expected, children of different households had various ideas about the future of the business, so natural conflicts began to surface.

The elders sent the message that peace was to be preserved at all costs and that the conservative ways were to be preferred. The family's old-line reputation within the community and the industry was to be upheld, with no hint of dissension affecting the family's honor. The younger generation felt they could not use their educations to make a difference. They began looking for ways to leave the business, feeling there was no place for their new ideas.

FAMILY AND THE ENTERPRISE

Collective Harmony tradition emphasizes family influence over business culture, as the enterprise is an extension of the family and its natural authority. Employees have their own place and roles within the family enterprise in exchange for their loyalty and fulfillment of the family's values.

Notably, family mission statements and company values statements — considered *de rigueur* these days in family business consulting — actually arose long ago in Harmony cultures to capture the values of family enterprises.

Mogi Family: Rules to Live By[27]

An enduring example of family enterprise values comes from the Mogi Family of Japan who established the seasoning company Kikkoman as one of the first global brands. The following principles, drawn from a longer list developed for their business 1500 years ago, epitomize Collective Harmony views:

> Make strong morals your foundation, and focus on money last.
>
> Strive for harmony in your family.
>
> Avoid luxury: a simple life is a virtuous life.
>
> Do the job that you were born to do, and only that job.
>
> Competition can help you get ahead, but do not compete unfairly or to an extreme.
>
> Eat the same food as your servants.
>
> Be strict with yourself, but be kind to your servants.
>
> Keep your personal expenses low.

Use the rest of your money for the good of the community to a level in keeping with your circumstances.

Keep track of your finances, and save money for the unexpected.

Have a family reunion twice a year. At these reunions, don't judge your family members based on their income, but rather on their character.

CHALLENGES OF COLLECTIVE HARMONY

The greatest strength of Collective Harmony is its connectedness, which fosters security, stability, predictability, and social support. These also create its greatest challenges, which are innovation and change. The elder generation may hold too tightly to their traditional ideas and discourage the open communication and collaboration so necessary for adaptation in a rapidly changing world. Holding to tradition may leave fewer options for handling crises or seizing opportunities. The younger generation may in turn be reticent about speaking up and sharing feelings or ideas with parents and elders.

Difficult Choices at a Fork in the Road

A Japanese family has run a successful resort for more than forty generations, with each successor taking the family name. The family has suffered the tragic death of their chosen family successor. His unmarried sister faces pressure to marry a man who can take on the title. But the family despairs because, after hundreds of years, they do not have a mechanism to move forward flexibly in the modern world.

Without the capacities of open communication, explicitness, and shared decision-making, families may find themselves stuck in a web of silent frustration. This was articulated well by a son from an Asian family, a young man raised and educated with Individualist influences before embarking on a career as a venture capitalist. Asked to return and help run his family's huge, global business, he described trying to cope with the slow pace of change in this tradition-bound culture:

> I think what has happened in Asia is not unique to this family, but a lot of Asian families, I think they face a couple of issues that the Western families don't face. And one of them I call, "Confucian causes confusion," meaning Confucian culture. The reason it causes confusion is that they want to keep everything confidential, it's "respect your elders." It's hard to really float up the key issues for discussion.[28]

The massive wave of family enterprise transitions in China and Hong Kong today is emblematic of these challenges. When China began permitting private enterprise and ownership after 1979, substantial family enterprises sprang forth to help forge modern East Asian entrepreneurship and economic development. The founders of those businesses are quintessential immigrants to wealth, having made the *Journey Up* most successfully.

Those families are now facing their first generational transition in leadership. They have no clear history or well-defined template for how to make this transition, with few knowledgeable peers they can turn to for guidance. They have as resources their advisors, split between Harmony-culture advisors with moderate experience and Individualist-trained advisors seeking to apply Western models. They have Confucian traditions, which worked well in a purer, more insulated cultural heritage but may be less applicable in a multicultural world. Otherwise, they are mostly guessing.

These prototypical Collective Harmony families are struggling with generational transition for the very reasons predicted by a cultural model. First, they are held back by their communication patterns. Not being able to discuss matters openly, elders cannot employ the main avenue used by most families for airing and resolving the dilemmas of transition. Second, their single-leadership model allows the family to draw from few of the many options for next-generation leadership of a large enterprise. They seek to replicate what they have rather than try innovative yet foreign governance models already in use in other cultures. Finally, their demand for keeping conflict subdued in the name of harmony limits creative input from a new generation excited to participate as equals in the enterprise.

MOVING FORWARD

At the same time there are generational stresses, major new developments are occurring in Collective Harmony. East Asian culture is undergoing significant change in the modern world. The Asia-Pacific region — growing to over 4.6 million high-net-worth individuals as of 2014 — is the fastest growing area of wealth development globally.[29] More so than in any previous time in history, the social traditions in Asian business are experiencing profound transformation as entrepreneurship takes hold across emerging markets.

Collective Harmony culture appears to be in the midst of loosening some of its traditional attitudes and behaviors related to communication, decision-making, collaboration, and the relative balance of the individual and the collective. Individual achievement may be bringing change to the region as never before, with glimmers appearing of greater capacity for direct communication and tolerating conflict. Though stressful, this may bode well for the family dynamics of enterprises within the Collective Harmony culture.

CHAPTER 6

Honor Culture

Many societies around the world operate within a traditional culture centered on the family and community, characterized by a fixed, elaborate, and ordered social hierarchy. This culture is essentially an extension of tribal society. The Honor cultural tradition remains predominant in Southern, Eastern and Central Europe, a residue of clans and royal courts; Central and South America; the Middle East and Africa; Russia; and, India, with colonial influences overlaid from Western Individualist culture.

Honor culture in fact is the original culture underpinning all other cultures. Harmony culture evolved from Honor culture in East Asia, while Individualist culture emerged in Britain and Northern Europe before spreading throughout Western society. Within Individualist cultures, there remain ethnic subcultures that more completely exhibit Honor roots. These include Hispanic subcultures as well as the Irish and Scottish clans of the United Kingdom, whose descendants in the American South demonstrate even to this day a genetic reactivity to grievances.[30]

A SOCIAL ORGANIZATION PROVIDING PROTECTION

A hallmark of Honor cultures is the hierarchically-organized social structure. The clan is embedded within a political structure based on relationships, with a culture of royalty, hereditary titles, and rulers overseeing social and commercial communities. Many Honor societies contend with instability in the governments surrounding them. With frequently shifting external governance structures resulting in wavering rule of law, families and tribes learned to manage themselves and their vulnerable members. As a result, clans and communities provide stability, trust, authority, and accountability within environments of risk.

In Honor culture the family is the social and economic focus of life, organized as a fixed hierarchy of obligation and role. More than an emphasis on harmony, there is respect for authority. Families are led by strong leaders who may be loved but are as likely to be feared and certainly obeyed. The status hierarchy is accepted, and one's place is clear from birth. Religious authority contributes significant elements of tradition and often provides more community bonds than the rapidly shifting governments who happen to be in power.

Honor cultures maintain strict boundaries between trust of one's own group and distrust of others. The Honor leader perceives and presents his social group as exceptional while dismissing others as less worthy, wrong, or even evil. He (and it is usually a male figure) projects power, is reactive to slights and wrongs, and attacks when feeling threatened rather than reaching out cooperatively. Paramount is defending one's power and authority and securing loyalty within one's group.

Women are generally respected and worshiped in Honor culture, though traditionally women have had a limited authority role until only recently. There have been powerful female political leaders in Honor countries, such as Indira Gandhi, Isabel Martinez de Peron, Christina Kirchner, Benazir Bhutto, and Golda Meir. Nevertheless, male leadership has tended to prevail in these largely male-dominated societies.

A Latin American Family with Strong Traditions[31]

A 120-year-old South American business conglomerate contains several dozen family members and nearly ten large businesses, ranging from entertainment to agribusiness to information technology. The family began five generations ago in retailing, as immigrants often do when they enter a new country. With each emerging generation, they expanded into new geographic territories and new businesses. Family members have been encouraged to migrate further to find fresh opportunities. Originating in one country, the family's reach now extends throughout three continents.

The family follows a traditional Honor structure. In their home country, the family lives together and all businesses are owned in common. Family members receive a salary according to their age, whether they work in the business or not. Working in the business does not lead to any extra income, so family members work for the challenge and prestige of their accomplishments.

Each business division has a family leader, its own board, and a strategy committee. Members of the family who work in the enterprise meet together and make decisions about business ventures. The eldest male family member is the head of the extended family and the overall decision-maker, especially in areas concerning the family.

Status in the family is based upon business position and contribution. The family has a Code of Conduct that governs financial income and business practices, enforced by the overall family leader. There are informal rules that no more than three active family partners may reside in any one country, that women will not work in the business, and that a family member will retire in his 60s and focus on philanthropy. These rules are enforced according to the level of authority of the family leader.

IDENTITY BASED ON RELATIONSHIP AND REPUTATION

The identity of the individual, as in Collective Harmony culture, is strongly socially determined. Self-worth is inextricably linked to honor and reputation — of oneself and of the family. Because of this, reputation must be constantly monitored, nurtured, protected, and defended. One's membership in the clan influences personal attributes such as social class, level of respect, sense of belonging, and degree of vulnerability. Career choice, academic achievement, and, in traditional families, marital options are evaluated by the impact on the collective family. Excessive self-determination and independence are suspect. They are seen as potentially dishonorable and disrespectful to the family, its reputation, and therefore its honor.

Because Honor culture emphasizes social class and status hierarchy, families (and family enterprises) often possess a highly political culture based on one's relationship with those in power. Tradition rules in Honor culture, with titles or hierarchical status passed down across generations. Hereditary prerogatives, titles, castes, and nobility endure. Change is slow in this world of chivalry and honor, of ritual and cultural celebrations. But change can occur if led by those in power.

Honor culture shares elements of the tradition-based Harmony style in its emphasis on respect, influence, social connectedness, and loyalty.

Collective Harmony's concept of "face" inhabits the Honor culture's valuing of reputation and respect. It lives in affirmative behaviors of paying respect to those in power and in avoidance of actions that may lead to dishonor, shame, humiliation, and loss of prestige. However, Honor culture depends less on shared maintenance of respect and more on the actions of individuals and families to claim respect and enforce their position of status. As such, it is more competitive than collaborative in maintaining the self-worth of its constituents.

INDIRECT COMMUNICATION, YET EMOTIONAL EXPRESSIVENESS

Honor culture is less preoccupied with harmony than the East Asian cultures with a similar family emphasis. Despite its similar reliance on moderate ambiguity in communication, Honor culture is more political and socially expressive. It can seem a volatile culture where conflicts are played out in high drama. The classic movie *The Godfather*[32] is a powerful depiction of an Honor culture family enterprise, played out in the New World. The story contains strong Honor culture themes: absolute devotion to the patriarch, a strict hierarchy based on family roles, trust and commitment flowing to those known and loyal to the family, safety and security within the clan to protect from the many dangers outside.

Straddling Two Cultures[33]

The patriarch in a Russian family from Belarus rose above very difficult circumstances to become a successful self-made real estate developer, achieving a certain level of power among other Russian wealth-creators and oligarchs. As is common, however, he sent his children and wife to the US to protect his family from some of the risks in Russia. They have become embedded in Western life; his children are now prominent professionals in business, law, and finance.

The father has great skills for managing the insular, almost tribal business environment back in Russia. Trust is built on relationships over long periods of time, whom you know is critical, and circles of power are very hard to break into. Maintaining one's reputation is crucial, as is the ability to navigate the closed byzantine bureaucracy that manages everything. There is a strong degree of nationalistic pride, which people in the

West do not really grasp. When the patriarch comes to the US for visits he straddles both worlds in his cultural skills and behaviors.

The family is now contemplating what to do about the wealth, the business back in Russia, and who has the ability to take over. The father has gradually opened up to discussing these issues with his grown children. But his view is that they are not ruthless enough to survive in the Russian business environment and culture. The family lives two lives: a business life in Honor culture and a family life in Individualist culture. Soon they must decide how to blend the two, or let go of one.

TRUST, TRANSPARENCY, AND LEADERSHIP

Leadership and decision-making within an Honor culture are typically strong, solo, and unchallenged, arising from prior protective leaders who were chief or king. Power adheres to those who are closest to the leader, leading to a relationship-based power structure. Decisions rely on consultative relationships for input but ultimately flow from a central power structure. Transparency is moderate, depending on one's place in the hierarchy. The inner circle may know quite a bit, but outsiders may have little input and receive little sharing of information.

The Experience of a Fifth-Generation Member in a Latin American Family[34]

A young fifth-generation (G5) family member related his developmental journey within the Latin American family enterprise. He was exposed to the business life of the family first by observing meetings at home and then by working summers and vacations in various divisions. He went north to be educated in American schools and was employed at a venture capital firm for ten years before returning to join the family business. As is often the case in this family, the G5 was mentored by one of his uncles upon entering one of the businesses. He advanced by identifying a manufacturing operation needing renewal, led a turnaround effort there, and greatly expanded that business. He has since worked at several other business divisions in various countries.

This successful G5 values the traditions and wide scope of the family enterprise as well as the many positions and status it offers him. He acknowledges that the policy of allowing any male family member to work in the business, whether they are capable or not , is something that probably needs to be evaluated and changed.

The family stays connected through a network of trust among the family members who work in the businesses. The large extended family, while emotionally close and participating in occasional whole-family gatherings, has been neglected in recent years compared to the enterprise. But those who work in the business are tightly bound and confer regularly in various capacities.

With so much contact with global business and other cultures, the family is experiencing increasing pressure to reconsider its longstanding policies about women, compensation, and governance. How they weather the next twenty years may determine the future of this traditional Honor-based family.

The differences between the hierarchies in the Harmony and Honor cultures lie in two areas. First, the social hierarchy in Honor culture is steeper, giving the family leader more power and discretion which are less hampered by tradition. There is less delegation down the ladder and less continuity in how authority is exercised. As in Harmony culture, succession often passes to the next generation by birth order or family position, most traditionally to males but with increasing involvement of women in the modern era. Leadership typically either continues the solo leadership model or cleaves the enterprise into branches led by single leaders. However, succession may be more disruptive as each new leader establishes his imprint on the family.

The second difference is that, without the stability conveyed by long tradition, the Honor culture hierarchy is more unstable and prone to discord. The leader can be challenged and deposed; alliances and conspiracies can take root. As a result, trust is fragile. There is a small circle of trust for those well-known to the family and the leadership. Trust is based only somewhat on what one does; trust is based much more on who one knows and their history of connection to the clan. Loyalty can be overcome by personal agendas and new alliances, but always with suspicion. An Honor family uses known networks because a trusted partner is hard to come by.

How Do I Trust You? Let Me Count the Ways

The divergent approaches to building trust in cultures are evident in an article[35] describing deal-making negotiations between companies in India (from the Honor culture) and Germany (from the Individualist style). The Indian company kept sending back the Germans' very clear and highly detailed proposals with questions about various points. A cross-cultural understanding would recognize that, rather than questioning the details of the agreement, the Indian company was using the negotiations to build trust by relationship. They were drawing out the "getting-to-know-you" period in order to deepen trust for the eventual alliance. The German firm only felt offended by all the nitpicking and what they saw as an apparent lack of trust. They assumed that clearly defining each party's interests via details of the agreement would create trust. Negotiations are often where cultural differences are played out, based on unspoken yet deeply-held underlying assumptions.

Many of the qualities of Honor culture can be understood by the fundamental experience of having to survive within conditions of instability. Without effective rule of law and reliable protection, people learn to protect themselves and their loved ones. They establish mechanisms of trust, guard information carefully, plan for succession precipitated by calamity, and react to real or perceived threats swiftly and decisively. Even seemingly unproductive behaviors like aggressively over-responding to perceived slights make sense from an Honor perspective. If one considers it better to strike early and hard to fend off potentially greater attacks later, each insult must be met with a strong response.

CHALLENGES OF THE HONOR CULTURE

Limitations of the Honor culture stem from its steep hierarchy based on authority and lack of tolerance for questioning or change using established governance procedures. Like in Harmony culture, families can overemphasize stability and may not permit change easily. Unless the family is more open and tolerant of adaptation, innovators struggle to have a voice. New ideas and new leaders find building trust to be difficult; they must first develop status and credibility within the family hierarchy.

Another drawback of the model is lack of transparency and the intense privacy with which information is held. The leader and the few whom he trusts may know what is happening, while others are kept in the dark. The inability to discuss plans or problems in a collaborative manner means that those lower in the hierarchy have few options but to wait respectfully and hope the future works out. The opaque nature of governance can breed frustration and ultimately lead to revolutionary rather than evolutionary transitions.

Honor culture is also prone to behind-the-scenes competition, where next-generation family members struggle for power and influence. These families can be highly—even destructively—competitive. Power is a prize, and apparent cooperation may simply cover jockeying for control. Alliances do not necessarily equal real collaboration. In addition, there is the ever-present risk from external influences and intrusive governments to guard against. Truly shared governance, open communication, and enduring collaborative leadership across branches and generations remain rare in Honor family enterprises.

An exceptional example today is unfolding in Russia where, as in China, a major cohort of capitalist wealth-creators is facing its first generational succession.[36] The fall of the Soviet Union in the 1980s led to an unprecedented wave of business entrepreneurship reaping significant wealth. Those entrepreneurs are now reaching the age where they normally would be looking to transfer their holdings to the next generation. However, the difficulty of passing on necessary business relationships, plus the risk that the government will seize the assets of the enterprise, is leading nearly half of surveyed owners to plan to exit rather than pass their businesses on to children.[37] In Harmony cultures, the risk to families comes from within, due to difficulties with communication and leadership. In Honor cultures, danger may arrive from the outside as well.

DRAWING TOGETHER THE CULTURES

Having clarified the general characteristics of the three main cultures, let us now summarize their qualities and transition to understanding the journeys of family enterprises.

CHAPTER 7

Comparison of the Three Cultural Styles

Table 7-1 summarizes common features of the three cultural styles along various dimensions important for understanding family enterprises:

Why the Three Cultures Matter

Understanding the Individualist, Collective Harmony, and Honor cultures is crucial for understanding the transitions and dilemmas that prominent family enterprises encounter.

Cultural styles tend to be purer and more entrenched at the foundations of the economic ladder. Families cope with economic adversity and scarcity using long-established patterns of communication, governance, values, family orientation, and openness to change. They may have less exposure to outside cultures as they go about their lives in local regions. The family's nature along key dimensions — such as the balance of the individual versus the collective — is a core part of their identity, their functioning, and their world-view.

The very act of becoming affluent and successful stresses families, requiring them to make adaptations in their traditions and their functioning. Starting from difficult, adverse economic circumstances, families first make the *Journey Up* the ladder of economic success. They then face the prospect of making the *Journey Across,* from their heritage traditions to the modern blended culture typical of significant family enterprises.

We will now examine those journeys, why they can be so stressful, and what can help families adapt to their new landscape successfully.

	Honor	Individualist	Collective Harmony
Primary Purpose of the Family	Respect tradition and authority within the family, whose power protects and sustains its members	Develop individuals to lead fulfilling lives	Maintain family relationships; fulfill obligation to sustain harmony and respect tradition within the family
Identity and Self-worth	Derived from one's own reputation, the family reputation, and one's role within the extended family hierarchy	Created predominantly by oneself, with some social determinants	Derived from and maintained by the family and the community, subservient to the family and its needs
Hierarchy/Status	Strong, fixed social hierarchy; clear differences among family members based on traditional roles	During childhood, hierarchy based on generation and birth order; adult family members are essentially equal	Hierarchal decision-making and relationships; individuals are to respect their place within the family and the organization
Trust	Built on strength of relationships and tradition, enhanced by personal evidence of trustworthiness over time	Based on individual performance and reliability in tasks when called upon; initially assumed to be present until otherwise disproven	Built through connection of relationships, affiliated groups/families; strong community and orientation to clan
Decision-making	Trust and power derive from one's relationship to the leader; individuals are not to question authority but should accept decisions; family members are to be taken care of by benevolent authority	Principle of "everyone has a right to be heard"; greater prevalence of collaborative or consensus decisions; decisions are supposed to be fair to everyone; "one voice, one vote"	Family members respect elders who are responsible for promoting wisdom; leaders are to act responsibly and wisely on behalf of the family

Comparison of the Three Cultural Styles

	Honor	Individualist	Collective Harmony
Basis for Decisions	Tradition more likely than data to determine resolution; general solutions may be implemented with details less important	Analytical, data-driven approach to decisions; timeliness and action are prized	Wisdom of tradition and traditional principles are used to overcome conflicts; long-term focus, patience in problem-solving
Transparency, Sharing of Ideas	Little transparency or sharing, especially with outsiders; sharing is possible only with those one knows well within the family	Transparency about family business is advocated; general ethic is to speak up and share one's ideas; innovation and new ideas are valued democratically	Little transparency; business details are held by leader, not shared; speaking up by family members is discouraged; feelings are kept veiled or revealed indirectly
Communication	Ambiguous and political, based on one's rank in the hierarchy	Business operations and agreements are rational, task-based, explicit, and oriented to work performance	Ambiguous and indirect in order to preserve "face" and not bring shame or embarrassment to anyone
Expression of Emotions	Communication with those one trusts can be direct and emotional, even volatile, otherwise cautious and hidden	Direct, rational; not supposed to be overly emotional, especially in business; open expression of feelings accepted in personal relationships	Emotion is controlled and to be demonstrated through action, not expressed directly

Table 7-1: Characteristics of the three cultural styles

SECTION II

The Journey Up, the Journey Across

CHAPTER 8

The Journey Up

We initially proposed a cultural perspective for understanding families of wealth and family enterprises a decade ago. In a 2007 *Journal of Wealth Management* article on the psychology of wealth,[38] we outlined what has become known as the "Immigrants and Natives" model for understanding the generational dynamics in wealthy families.

Viewing families through their transitions in economic culture originated in an awareness of the demographics of wealth. Whether in developed or developing economies, the overwhelming majority of wealth-holders are new to wealth. Inherited wealth typically constitutes less than 10–15% of the wealth population, while those who are self-made or significantly growing what they inherited represent 75–85% of the wealthy. In fast-growing emerging markets (encompassing the Honor and Harmony cultures in today's world) the proportion of self-made wealth-creators to all wealth-holders approaches 90%, as wealth creation spreads at an unprecedented rate.[39] In China, a new billionaire emerges every month, meaning another newcomer to wealth has to find his or her way through an unfamiliar cultural realm.

Immigrants to Wealth

The overwhelming majority of the wealthy make a journey of migration over the course of their lifetime from an economic culture of scarcity to a culture of abundance. They are, in essence, "Immigrants to the Land of Wealth."[40] Their personalities, attitudes, beliefs, and behaviors were largely formed in the economic heritage of their upbringing, whether that was the middle class, the working class, or poverty.

It is important to understand families not just in terms of where they now are but where they first came from, economically. Since our model has gained traction within the financial services industry, recent demographic studies of the wealthy[41] have confirmed what our experience indicated: that most wealthy families emerge over the course of a lifetime from humble circumstances. Creating an affluent, successful family enterprise is a narrative of economic migration and cultural adjustment for families.

It is a *Journey Up* the economic ladder (Figure 8-1):

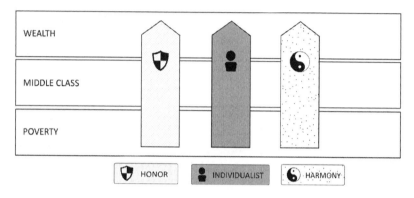

Figure 8-1: The Journey Up: Economic transition in family enterprises

The cultural journey for these economic immigrants in the first generation of wealth is transformative, for themselves and for the family. Acquirers of wealth share many characteristics of geographic immigrants, shaping the future life of the family. Generation One (G1) wealth creators tend to be entrepreneurial, hard-working, self-sufficient, independent, strong-minded individuals who can persevere in the face of risk and adversity. Particularly in Western society, they are avid believers in those qualities that define the Individualist character—individual initiative, assertion of dignity and self-worth, flexibility, directness in communication, logical thinking, and personal power. Interestingly, many of them are also true immigrants from other ethnic cultures who have courageously left difficult environments in pursuit of greater freedom and opportunity.

Even in Honor and Harmony cultures, hard-working entrepreneurs are typically strong-minded, able to assess and persevere in taking risk, and decisive. They are the leaders who bring the family to prosperity through great effort and strength. Their status comes from personal achievement in a culture rooted in traditional authority, which makes them unique.

THE OTHER SET OF WEALTH'S IMMIGRANTS

Families of wealth contain another set of economic Immigrants: the in-laws who marry in from non-wealthy families. In-law spouses from middle-class or working-class families also arise in a culture of scarcity, knowing little of the behaviors, language, or attitudes natural to wealth. They may not have the characteristics of those larger-than-life wealth creators; they may in fact be more fortunate than capable. But they are nevertheless immigrants to a new culture. They must adjust as best they can, given the mistrust often directed their way.

Implications of the Model

Two key insights naturally flow from recognizing that the majority of the wealthy are like "immigrants to wealth."

NATURAL-BORN CITIZENS OF THE LAND OF WEALTH

The first insight is that, unlike economic newcomers migrating to wealth, subsequent generations are more "native to wealth," influenced by their exposure to affluence during their formative years.[42] Wealth and success, particularly in family enterprises, represent their economic culture of origin. They learn the behaviors, attitudes, language, and perspectives of affluence from childhood. Their life experience is very different than G1 wealth creators:

- They know security and comfort rather than insecurity, scarcity, and the economic deprivation of their forebears. This impacts their perspectives and potentially their sense of security in the world. Unfortunately, it also may impact their competencies for handling adversity. In each of the three ethnic cultures, hiring servants at home and advisors for family affairs are often visible signs of the family's success. Many in Generations 2, 3, and beyond reach adulthood lacking certain life skills as a result of this insulation from responsibility. The pampered, dependent life of wealth's Natives may be a badge of honor for wealth creators, but it leaves many inheritors unprepared for managing life on their own. Others must develop these skills as adults using peer networks and other resources.

- Compared to their successful parents or grandparents, Natives of wealth may be envied but less respected. Societies around the world view inherited wealth as unearned and therefore undeserved. Those born to successful family enterprises may experience stereotyping, bias, and patronizing attitudes from general society. As heirs, they must contend with an image of being entitled, spoiled, and shallow, even if they have solid values and work hard in the family enterprise.

- Many Natives may be unskilled with whatever wealth they may own, due to being insulated and taken care of by advisors and family leaders. They may also have little true control over their wealth, due to the decisions of wealth-creators who tie up assets in trusts or other financial or legal entities.

The lives of wealth's Natives are very different than those of wealth's Immigrants. They arise within the culture of affluence as beneficiaries of the journey the family navigates, up the economic ladder.

PARENTING AND ADAPTATION

Secondly, the cultural model provides insight into the dilemmas of parenting across economic cultures. Just like geographic immigrants migrating to a new land to make a better life for the family, wealth's immigrants face dilemmas inherent in raising children and grandchildren in a foreign culture. How should parenting be adapted for the new circumstances? What still applies, and what must be changed? How and when are those changes to be implemented? The family dynamics of successful families and family enterprises in any ethnic culture have many characteristics in common with immigrant family dynamics, with some of the same questions, stresses, and adaptations necessary for the family to survive the transition.

Elders who achieve success may cling to methods of parenting that date from their own upbringing in a more modest economic level within the Individualist, Harmony, or Honor cultures. Those parenting methods may have been perfectly appropriate during times of adversity. Important aspects may be much less applicable in an environment of comfort.

A near-universal question we hear from G1 clients of all cultures is: "my children [or grandchildren] are growing up so much more comfortably than I did—how do I instill in them the values and the hard lessons fundamental to my success?" The transition from economic struggle to economic success challenges the teachings that must pass between the elder generation and their offspring. These teachings also include passing on traditions from their ethnic cultural heritage, traditions which may start to seem very distant to the next generation.

INDEPENDENCE AND INTERDEPENDENCE

As families make the *Journey Up*, two main skill sets must be fostered in order to produce responsible, purposeful members able to work together for the benefit of the family. One set of skills fosters the individual, or what we have called the competencies of *Independence*.[43] The other set fosters skills for collaboration and collective benefit of the family, or what we have called the competencies of *Interdependence*.

Independence: If affluent families focus at all on teaching wealth skills, they most often focus on teaching their children the skills of Independence. These include the following:

- Financial education for basic money skills—saving, spending, budgeting, managing credit and debt, keeping track of what one has, and related financial self-management skills
- Learning perseverance and a good work ethic, having initiative, being able to persist in purposeful tasks
- Contributing time, talent, or money to philanthropic causes
- Knowing how to work with advisors, including how to evaluate the trustworthiness of advisors and provide oversight for their activities
- Developing a stable, healthy identity as a person from a prosperous family; avoiding entitlement and the pitfalls of wealth which corrode identity and self-esteem
- Depending on the ethnic culture and jurisdiction, having

knowledge and skills to be a responsible beneficiary of trusts, including knowing how to work with trustees and to manage spending within appropriate distribution policies

- For most affluent generations, learning how to live simultaneously among the wealthy and within general society. Though the wealthy often live and work among others of similar economic level, most also inhabit a world with economic diversity to a greater or lesser extent. Navigating a diverse society means having skills for handling relationships with ease and tact, for understanding the daily stresses of economic adversity without necessarily experiencing them, and for working at tasks purposefully without necessarily having to make a living at it, alongside others who may have no choice in this.

These skills of affluent life are hard enough to develop. They can take a lifetime of effort to accomplish well. What is relevant is that their focus is largely devoted to the individual and his or her life purpose. The goal is to integrate the best aspects of the family's past economic heritage with the most positive elements from its current situation. That means being bicultural for wealth's Immigrants and Natives: holding on to traditional values and behaviors while taking on the new skills and behaviors of wealth.

Interdependence: When families share assets, however, a second set of skills is needed. A successful family enterprise must be able to function on a collective level due to the reality that its members are interdependent with each other.

The skills of Interdependence vary among the three ethnic cultures in important ways. In Individualist culture, family members must learn how to share decision-making utilizing the governance policies, procedures, and structures known to foster healthy family functioning. They must learn the values of stewardship, the legacy of the family's heritage, and the shared vision of the family enterprise. Interdependence requires skills for collaboration and negotiation around the family table, skills which may be lacking when everyone is more concerned with the welfare of themselves or just their branch of the family.

In Collective Harmony cultures, a delicate balance is required between the individual needs of family members and the collective needs of generations. Healthy Interdependence skills require the ability to balance directness and ambiguity, respectfulness and assertiveness. Family members must be able to share in problem-solving using holistic, context-rich thinking. They must find meaningful roles for each family member and engage them in family activities. They must know how to offer suggestions in highly tactful, gently respectful ways so that their views are more likely to be heard and (potentially) accepted. This way, the family can evolve together while remaining connected and aligned with tradition.

In Honor cultures, the family may be tied together strongly at the asset level but decision-making is likely to be embedded in authoritarian leadership. Healthy Interdependence skills allow for more collaboration and greater shared communication. Family members must know how to speak up respectfully within the privacy of the family leadership, offering their perspectives while not appearing to unduly challenge elders. Leaders must be able to reach out to family members who possess less power but have ideas, energy, or skills to contribute. These elders must have skills for listening and inviting input without seeing disrespect around every corner. Active, engaged, yet respectful debate is a key skill for Interdependence in Honor cultures, as they prepare for generational transitions in a changing cultural and business climate.

ME AND WE ACROSS THE GENERATIONS

These two categories of skills — Independence and Interdependence — are fundamental to successful families making the *Journey Up* within whatever ethnic culture they belong. There must be a healthy balance between the individual (the "Me") and the family (the "We") if the family is to adapt successfully from its humble roots.

There are important similarities and differences in the *Journey Up* in the three ethnic cultures. The Land of Wealth may look differently depending on the family's ethnic heritage. Let us examine each culture in greater depth before moving on to the second major adaptation faced by family enterprises.

CHAPTER 9

The Journey Up in the Three Cultures

A central challenge for all families in the *Journey Up* is coping with abundance after a heritage of scarcity. In the founders' background, resources were scarce, adversity spawned innovation, skills were crucial, and risks were high. Now, the family must adapt to a life of comfort. Wealth's Natives develop in an environment where resources are abundant, sometimes to the point of excess. Parenting changes when constraints on spending go away, when "No, we can't," no longer applies. Skills wither when children are insulated from life's responsibilities. Risks are minimized when money can solve most problems, or seem to.

In an environment of abundance, families must tackle different dilemmas: how to educate the next generation to handle wealth responsibly, how to make wise decisions about philanthropic endeavors, how to fulfill the family's values, and how to incorporate new members entering the family through marriage or affiliation. To a greater or lesser extent, these strains are endemic to the affluent level of any ethnic culture. Yet each culture has its own patterns and therefore its own dilemmas.

Individualist Cultures

In Western Individualist culture, wealth-creating family leaders embody the behaviors of the culture: assertiveness, directness, self-sufficiency and independence. Problems are handled and discussed in logical, analytical style. Decision-making is strong, sometimes autocratic. There is little ambiguity in expression from a cultural standpoint. If there is a need to read between the lines or tiptoe around potentially embarrassing issues, it comes from emotional avoidance rather than cultural norms. Yet, many patriarchs and matriarchs will appreciate a next-generation child or grandchild who speaks up assertively as being cut from the same cloth as themselves.

Conflict may be uncomfortable at times and many issues may remain unspoken or procrastinated. Nevertheless, assertiveness may be ultimately respected as strength rather than betrayal. Strong-minded first-generation patriarchs and matriarchs understand the necessity to foster skills for Independence in children and grandchildren. They see these skills as fundamental to their own success and to the development of the family enterprise itself.

The necessity to embrace and manage Interdependence is much more challenging for many Individualist families. Moving on from the authority of the first-generation founder, successful families may recognize intellectually that responsibility for wealth in the next generation should be shared. However, Individualist tradition tends to ignore those skills or emphasize competition among siblings more than cooperation.

Collaboration in Individualist cultures is more often framed in stewardship terms rather than governance terms. Families often envision interdependence in their philanthropy, for example; less so in their governance. They see their family foundation as a vehicle for developing next-generation competencies in cooperation and compromise, yet they shy away from developing a family council.

Many patriarchs get impatient sharing decisions with others less experienced in enterprise matters. They may disdain what they see as the slow, convoluted process of "decision-making by committee" when the family tries to work things out together. Founders may not even be sure that effective shared decision-making is possible, hearing horror stories of families who fought over assets after the first generation passed on. Their professional advisors may convince them that shared family governance is rarely successful, so why not just plan for professional management of assets held in partnerships or trusts? In truth, without thoughtful development of collaboration skills in the next generation, the failure to manage Interdependence becomes a self-fulfilling prophecy.

Trust "Maturity" — Going Our Own Way

An Individualist family with extensive real estate holdings faced the impending maturity and termination of a 120-year trust, administered by trustees operating as traditional financial stewards with little participation by the families. Regular substantial distributions had been made to the beneficiaries who generally worked in low-level jobs, sometimes in community service. The beneficiaries did not identify with each other or the extended family, other than sharing dependency on trust distributions for their livelihoods.

As the trust's termination approached, the expectation was that beneficiaries would all go their own ways, though the trustees pushed for the family to simply continue the trust as it had been (including dependency on the trustees). A few beneficiaries, cherishing sustainability and environmental responsibility, wanted instead to become more active owners and invest together according to their values. The trustees and other advisors derided them as naïve amateurs.

The process devolved into litigation without the different beneficiary groups becoming cohesive. There was no collective sense of heritage or tradition to help guide them. Other than receiving money distributed from the same pot, there was no future expectation of being connected in any way. They lacked a shared history and a set of competencies for working together.

Fortunately, the trend in family business consulting over the past thirty years has been to advocate for families' learning of Interdependence skills. Best practices now include prescriptions for working collaboratively on family constitutions, councils, mission statements, values exercises, policy development, communication ground rules, and related processes. These build cohesion and create methods for families who are interdependent in their assets to be interdependent in their actions.

INDIVIDUALIST FAMILIES WHO SUCCEED

Though strong single leadership remains the norm in Individualist families, increasing numbers of Western family enterprises have shifted to a more collaborative model of shared decision-making. These families reap the advantages of a broader menu of leadership and decision-making styles. They understand the benefits of family councils for balancing individual and shared values and goals, including development of policies and procedures that operate independently of whoever is sitting at the head of the table at any given time. Their governance models rely on many family voices rather than one leader's veto.

Some Individualist families make the journey to wealth naturally predisposed for these skills. These families have a built-in heritage of nurturing family cohesion, speaking directly and honestly with each other, maintaining respectful communication, and reaching consensus on decisions impacting the family. They carry this heritage with them from middle-class life as they make the economic *Journey Up*. They intuitively see the wisdom in enhancing their collective orientation — their "familiness"[44] — to help manage disputes.

Whether Western families are familiar with a collective/family orientation or not, our experience is that successful family enterprises must move toward a healthy balance between the Independence skills of each family member and Interdependence skills of the family. To benefit from the bounty of the family enterprise, the family must inevitably adapt itself toward balancing the individual and the collective.

Collective Harmony and Honor Cultures

In Collective Harmony and Honor cultures, the reverse pattern tends to prevail. As families ascend the economic ladder, they migrate to circumstances that are more affluent but not necessarily more individualistic. There remains a very strong focus on the family and the collective, with the individual having to fit within established roles, responsibilities, positions, and (not infrequently) life plans. Family harmony, hierarchical decision-making, loyalty to the patriarch, and obedience are highly prized. The voices of the next generation — with their new ideas or areas of disagreement — are less welcome.

These cultures traditionally elevate the group and the family so highly that strong individualism is a rare quality. Honor cultures may entertain some discussion about individual plans and desires, but their traditional emphasis is still on fitting into the needs of the clan and the enterprise. They value getting along rather than standing out.

Greater affluence also brings new risks to the family in the form of greater materialism and insulation from responsibility. In Collective Harmony culture, for example, families proudly employ servants within the household to take over menial tasks, assist with raising children, and generally support a life of leisure. A natural consequence is that children and grandchildren lose skills of self-sufficiency and initiative in their lives as "natives of the Land of Wealth." The family may be lulled into dissipating the very skills and values that helped the first generation rise above its circumstances of scarcity and adversity.

As noted in Chapter 8, it would be a mistake to assume that Honor and Harmony cultures are skilled at Interdependence and only need to emphasize Independence more. Although Honor and Harmony families may have a much deeper heritage in understanding collective family enterprises, they also have traditionally rigid systems of centralized leadership, closed communication, and enforced loyalty with suppressed dissent.[45] This means true skills for handling Interdependence are not widely dispersed throughout the family system. Honor and Harmony families in the modern world need to develop skills of shared governance and stewardship just as much as Individualist families do. They simply set out from a different direction.

A CHANGE IN TREND

Fortunately, just as modern Individualist families are learning to embrace Interdependence, there is a definite trend in Honor and Harmony cultures toward fostering more Independence of the individual. The rise of entrepreneurship in China, Singapore, and Hong Kong, for example, is creating a generation more attuned to its own inclinations and more willing to assert itself to achieve goals. Middle Eastern, Indian, Russian, and Latin American families are experiencing the same pressures and transitions. Societies in developing economies are accepting more individualism, initiative, and assertiveness as entrepreneurship takes hold.

As we shall explore in the following chapters, the children and grandchildren in Honor and Harmony cultures are creating culture change from another set of influences. Exposed to Individualist attitudes and behaviors during their education or early career jobs abroad, they return to the family enterprise sparked by the excitement of pursuing their own dreams and initiatives. They want to introduce notions of gender equality and opportunity, collaboration and transparency.

Honor and Harmony cultures are therefore experiencing their own transitions at the highest levels of affluence, once the family makes the *Journey Up*. One transition is a fundamental shift away from an emphasis on the family/collective toward greater support of Independence skills for individual family members. The other is a qualitative change in Interdependence skills from the traditional autocratic model to a more modern collaborative model.

Finding the Right Balance in Family Enterprises

Rather than seeing the dimension of individualism versus collectivism as a single axis with two poles, it may be more useful to view individualism and collectivism as two independent qualities present to greater or lesser degrees in various cultures. Family enterprises can be low or high on each of these dimensions, depending on their orientation and the effort they put into developing their skills and core values.

We propose that a necessary adaptation of all successful family enterprises is to grow toward healthy support of both the individual and the family, capturing that crucial balance between Independence and Interdependence (see Figure 9-1).

By creating a healthy balance between the individual and the collective family, family enterprises foster the complete set of skills needed to adapt across generations. The need for this becomes apparent as they make their most fundamental cultural transition, the *Journey Up* in economic prosperity.

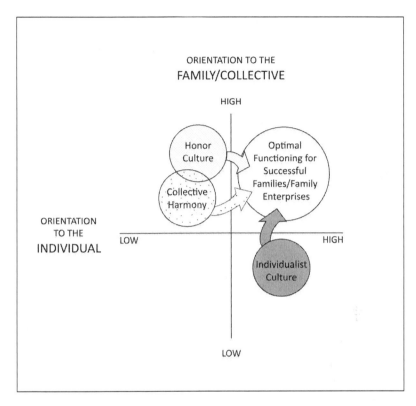

Figure 9-1: Patterns of orientation to the individual and the family/collective for the three global cultures, with optimal goal

Another Transition Awaits

The generational transition from Immigrants to Natives is a daunting challenge in the *Journey Up*. But there remains yet another transition awaiting successful families around the world. It is the *Journey Across* the broad landscape of global ethnic cultures.

CHAPTER 10

The Journey Across

As families reach the highest levels of economic security and social mobility, their members become exposed to a cultural blend comprised of elements from the three cultural models, plus a certain level of wealth. Wealthy business leaders maintain offices and apartments in different countries, bringing elements of their old culture with them while having to adapt to new surroundings. Wealthy families purchase international residences and spend time in business hubs such as London, Singapore, New York, Hong Kong, Miami, and Dubai. There, they interact with other successful individuals and families from diverse cultural traditions. Younger generations from Honor and Harmony cultures pursue education in Individualist secondary, undergraduate, and graduate schools.

As a result, in the past three decades, several forces have been intersecting in family enterprises to break down the longstanding barriers among ethnic cultures.

One is the ascendance of complex, regulated, competitive global businesses, requiring family enterprises to compete in a more challenging, unforgiving multicultural environment. This environment demands top-quality execution and offers fewer traditional protections. It also no longer allows family enterprises to remain sheltered within their own ethnic cultural environment.

Another factor is the changing cultural makeup of modern generations, impacted by the global, digital, comprehensive education provided to privileged youth from each of the three cultures. As younger family enterprise members circulate through institutions of privilege and education like bees through a garden, they inevitably pick up ideas and perspectives. They then return home to their family of origin bearing foreign influences. The dramatic exposure of wealth's natives to the wide world of global information has accelerated the tendency of younger generations to challenge and change cultural norms within their family. Their reception back home may not always be warm or welcoming. But their influence is undeniable.

The three cultural populations are therefore increasingly contacting each other via the flow of families through business, educational, social, and occupational channels around the world. Exposure to other cultures is the first step in precipitating change. But, change alone is merely stressful. Success in the modern world (with attendant increases in wealth) requires cross-cultural adaptation.

THE JOURNEY ACROSS: ENCOUNTERING THE
AMBICULTURAL BLEND

One commentator has stated that members of this affluent international culture are "a trans-global community of peers who have more in common with one another than with their countrymen back home."[46] This "ambicultural blend" has characteristics of its own, related to but separate from the three ethnic cultural styles.[47]

Figure 10-1 illustrates what happens when families achieve significant wealth and begin to encounter influences from cultures outside their own:

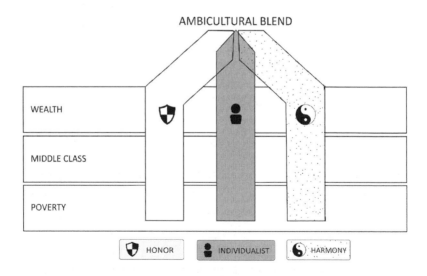

Figure 10-1: The Journey Across: Blending ethnic cultures in successful global families

As Figure 10-1 depicts, successful families with global exposure begin to take on language, attitudes, behaviors, and cultural awareness influenced by all three major cultural styles. Some observers[48] note that global modern businesses in Asia, Latin America, or the Middle East try to incorporate Western business practices alongside more collective traditions: greater social awareness, attunement to the needs of lower-income economies and populations, and greater attention to using established business networks than is typical in the West. There is greater acceptance of relationships that cross ethnic and racial lines, greater knowledge of several languages (with English predominating), significant cross-border travel experience, and knowledge of customs in multiple countries and cultures.

Two Global Families Face Journeys Up and Across (Part 3 of 4)

Simón Borrego and his father Juan went through a deep chill in their relationship that was only resolved by the intervention of his father's brother. The uncle understood the complexities of the global opportunities Simón faced, and he had the benefit of his brother's trust despite the pain of the family rift. Gradually, over several private meetings, the three men negotiated a new role for Simón. It respected his outside interests and responsibilities while preserving a place for his wise counsel within his family. Simón became part of a newly-formed family council within his family, and he held a position on the board overseeing the Borrego business interests. As a result, he traveled to Spain three times a year to participate in his own family's interests, accompanied by Vanessa and their young children.

Establishment of the family council did not go smoothly. The patriarch Juan struggled with the council's need for information sharing, setting of policies independent of the person at the head of the table, and the time devoted to discussion that (in Juan's view) could've been handled more efficiently by his just making the decision. In turn, the council strove to honor the patriarch but remained firm in establishing their own authority. Over a seven-year period the family gradually grew into their new process. As a result, the Borrego Family began to diversify out of steel and manufacturing into finance, real estate, and wealth management.

In Hong Kong, the working relationship between Wen Ho and Simón Borrego also went through transitions due to their cultural differences. Educated in London, Simón had learned to speak up about questions, issues, and reactions as a normal part of communicating with peers and authorities. He also was used to a more active give-and-take with a family leader like his father. Wen Ho experienced Simón's communication style as aggressive and challenging.

Vanessa had to mediate with each of them, helping them not take their differences personally. Now an advisor to the business about fabric styles within fashion trends, she herself grew to blend cultural attitudes respecting Chinese traditionalism, Western assertiveness and women's rights, and Latin preoccupation with family honor and reputation.

One of Simón's frustrations was in dealing with the savvy but impassive Wen Ho, who negotiated business deals in a manner that left seemingly crucial details unspecified (according to Simón and many Western business partners). Simon also had to accept rebukes from Wen Ho when he made mistakes in protocol when dealing with business partners or social acquaintances. But their mutual respect and the bonds of family helped the relationship prosper. With it, the business flourished and the family's wealth increased. They had risen far from the farming villages where Wen Ho and Li-Peng were born. They were beginning to surpass the Borrego enterprise as a global business.

FUSION VERSUS HYBRID BLENDING

Jeanne Brett and her colleagues have aptly described the possibilities in blending of cultures using the analogy of "hybrid" versus "fusion" cooking.[49] Hybrid blending combines features of two or more styles, adding in specific qualities from one culture to the fundamental nature of another culture. The styles in a fusion blend are truly intermixed to create a new culinary or cultural experience. What gets created reflects the component styles but is different from any one style.

In a hybrid family culture, a family adopts new cultural elements alongside their heritage traditional ways. This is what often happens when families in Harmony or Honor cultures try to adopt Individualist recommendations such as a family council, egalitarian voting rights, or a family constitution. The success of such endeavors depends greatly on how much the family truly grasps the reasoning behind the practice and tries to adopt the cultural perspectives involved.

Ambiculturalism is more like a fusion approach, where the old and new cultures coalesce into a blend where neither one predominates. Although individuals and families still clearly identify with a home country or culture, their identity begins to shift to being a global citizen with greater cultural intelligence. With "more in common with one another than with their countrymen back home"[50] they are often more relaxed and comfortable with other globally-aware citizens than with peers or family who only know one culture, one home. As one third-generation leader of a South American family, whose grandparents had emigrated from Japan, described her leadership style, she "had Japanese hardware and South American software." She assisted the older generation in communicating more and overcoming their reluctance to deal with manageable conflict.

We believe that migration into this blended culture is greater from the Collective Harmony and Honor cultures than from Individualist culture. Global business increasingly incorporates Individualist principles and procedures as a result of corporate governance requirements, the use of English as the language of trade, and the necessity to understand Individualist practices in commerce. Similarly, global travel and education expose younger generations to Western perspectives with their powerful emphasis on the individual, diluting the influence of the family.

As a result, the stresses on Harmony and Honor families are greater and the solutions required for those families are more complex. However, even families from Individualist culture encounter change when, for example, next-generation members press for greater attention to collective governance, much to the dismay of their first-generation patriarchs.

The Ly Family: Success Blending Cultures[51]

The five brothers of the Ly family were farmers who originated in China but immigrated to Vietnam. They later fled that country for America as "boat people" in the 1970s. Arriving without money or language skills, the Ly brothers seized the best opportunity they could find in their new country: opening a donut shop. They carried with them their values about the primacy of family and of everyone working hard in the new business. Over time they bought shops for each of the brothers, operating the growing family business according to their Confucian values.

Eventually, in a break from tradition, the Ly brothers selected the visionary middle brother rather than the eldest to pursue further education. He then identified opportunities for the family in food manufacturing, but he required the support of the family for his initiatives. Influenced by Individualist principles and perspectives, his brothers slowly learned to become comfortable with his leadership. He guided the family into developing a substantial enterprise. By tradition, members of the next generation all entered the business. They trained for various roles as needed and worked together in harmony. They have now crafted a blend of Asian business principles with new management strategies from Western Individualist tradition.

Confirmation from Emerging Research

New research currently underway—the Hundred Year Family Enterprise research project[52]—provides substantial support for the blended cultural model we see emerging. In this extensive ongoing project under the direction of one of us (Dennis Jaffe), members are interviewed from two generations within over eighty large, global family enterprises who have made it to their third or later generation. The purpose is to discover the factors underlying longevity and success in those family enterprises which have prospered rather than failed.

Many of the principles outlined in our model are emerging as key contributors to how families navigate the journey successfully both Up and Across. These families adapt progressively in each generation, and they are highly engaged in learning across generations. They form a cross-generational community open to talking with each other about new directions. They also typically strive over generations to create a healthy balance of skills for Independence and Interdependence within the family.

In their interviews, these families describe specific stress points, generational conflicts, and culture clashes encountered along the way. Their experiences underscore the themes families face as they rise toward the blended culture of global affluence.

Luen Thai: A Harmony Culture Family Enterprise[53]

For over three generations, the Tan family (no relation to the author Amy Tan) has lived in various places in South Asia, working together to develop a huge global conglomerate with interests in shipping, travel, hotels, airlines, real estate, insurance, and information technology. From humble beginnings in China, Dr. Tan Siu-lin, his wife Lam Pek-kim, their five sons, and one son-in-law have created a thriving portfolio of businesses and a strong spirit of cooperation within the whole family, extending now toward the fourth generation.

While each individual develops skills, the intention is to serve the family rather than find one's own way in life. With expectations that each member of the family will contribute to the enterprise, every G2 son, plus the son-in-law, entered the business with a particular area of interest. Each served an apprenticeship then worked in an existing business, ultimately developing one business in which they achieved leadership. Family members are encouraged in general to start and develop new businesses for the family.

Dr. Tan exemplifies Harmony culture in his values and the assumption that family is the foundation for everything. Every family member has a role, with constant attention to the whole clan:

"Focus is important. Being focused and hands-on, people would be able to appreciate the fruits [of their labor] as they nurture them with dedication. As each of us has different strengths, by complementing each other and working together in unity, we will draw the synergy and multiplier effect."[54]

From the beginning, the family was strongly rooted in traditional values, proposed by Dr. Tan:

- Live with loyalty and honesty, steer the family with hard work and thrift.
- Uphold filial piety and brotherhood.
- Develop yourself and set your life goal with an internal drive.
- Work together to build the family foundation.
- Serve the community and glory to the ancestor.
- Remember and follow this precept.

The family culture is consciously frugal. They make modest salaries and live modest lifestyles for their economic status. They emphasize service and work, with the family in the center. Money and ownership are managed together, with everyone receiving benefits from a family trust. The family as a whole is now setting up philanthropic ventures. Every week, there is a family dinner that everyone attends if they are in town.

Influences on the Journey Across

Just as there are predictable strains in the *Journey Up* for families, there are easily identifiable influences encountered during the *Journey Across*. These create common developmental challenges as the family attempts to resolve issues about the future of the family, the family enterprise, and how to use its many resources.

EDUCATION

The very act of sending children and grandchildren off to Individualist countries for education — a badge of wealth and upward mobility in many Harmony or Honor families — insures exposure to Individualist thinking for those generations. Students learn the broad spectrum that exists in communication, leadership, analysis, problem-solving strategies, business models, family patterns, and management styles across cultures. This may begin as early as private secondary school, and it may continue throughout college and post-graduate education.

Individualist Influences Begin Early

A teenage student from a wealthy Korean family attends an elite New England preparatory school in the United States. Like many of his peers, he sometimes dozes off in class, does not always apply himself to his homework, and lets his grades slip. He is referred to the school psychologist to see what the problem may be. During counseling sessions, the student begins to speak up about common adolescent issues related to academic pressure, family stress, and uncertainties about future goals. The psychologist listens sympathetically. She encourages the young teenager to think for himself and to take his time evaluating all his options about life, even if it takes years through college and beyond.

In an international phone call to the psychologist to discuss progress, the boy's Korean mother emphasizes it is important to the family that the student work hard, maintain good grades, and gain acceptance to a prominent American university. Consistent with Korean culture, he is to eventually take his predestined place in the family's industrial enterprise. The family needs him there, and his future is clear. Much goes unspoken out of politeness and an indirect, high-context communication style. The mother naturally assumes the psychologist shares the cultural imperative that the family takes precedence over the individual.

After a few unsuccessful attempts to explain it may not be so simple, the psychologist pacifies the mother by assuring her that progress is being made. The psychologist later tells a colleague, "oh, those 'Tiger Moms'! They just don't understand." She goes back to her counseling sessions with the teen, seeing herself as a liberator of another young mind. The psychologist does not fully grasp her role in introducing the Korean student to the ways of Individualist culture, with potential long-term implications for the family and its enterprise.

In college entrepreneurship courses, students learn about innovation practices that may not be common in their family enterprises. Their business school education will be steeped in individualism. In fact, international students may not even be admitted to prestigious graduate business programs unless they already demonstrate they can be assertive, articulate, and ready to explore challenging ideas. Passive, obedient students don't get past the gates of such programs.[55] When called upon in class, students will be expected to share their ideas openly and creatively, often without regard to how compliant they are with the professor's views. These experiences teach students new cultural norms about speaking up and challenging elders, rather than continuing traditions of respect through silence.

In courses about empathy training, emotional intelligence, and negotiation, Harmony and Honor students explore apparently radical notions like open expression of feelings, tolerance of conflict, and resolution of differences by collaborative discussion. They learn team building and trust building in small-group breakouts. They experience democratic, gender-neutral, nonhierarchical discussion and decision-making. In these same programs, students from Individualist cultures learn to notice and become adept with subtle social cues and layers of meaning. They begin to grow skills for handling ambiguity and context.

Young members from Harmony and Honor cultures also experience the potent impact of being mentored by Individualist teachers and professors. Those educators encourage attention to the self, speaking up (without fear of shame or punishment), and that ultimate in Individualist ideals, "the pursuit of your passions." These will all prove to be transformative to the student. They also contain the seeds of revolution for the family enterprise.

The Dilemma of Obligation

An early-twenties Asian student goes to an elite preparatory school and Ivy League university, supported by his family's extensive resources. As he prepares to graduate, his father (raised in poverty in China) asks him to return home and work for the business, with the eventual goal of taking over leadership. This request bypasses the older daughter who already has obtained an MBA and is working in management quite successfully.

The son feels he is not ready to do as his father asks. He wants to pursue an MBA degree and get experience working elsewhere in the industry first. His father says, "Why do you need to work outside? We will teach you what you need to know."

The son feels the tug of obligation but does not yet want to return to a manufacturing city inside China, find a wife, and make a family there. He also is sensitive to his sister's feelings and wishes for her to be included in the discussions. The father, however, does not feel it is proper to talk as a family. He only communicates one-on-one with his son. The son is not sure how to tell his father about his ambivalence over the plan; he feels there is no way out. This ambicultural son faces an inner conflict between respecting his new-found individual self or his longstanding family tradition.

Even Individualist students may be changed toward a more ambicultural perspective by their education. Coming from an autocratic family espousing individualism while stifling dissent, a young student can be exposed to families with greater focus on collective family qualities and Interdependence: best practices about governance, collective shared decision-making, greater freedom of expression, healthy respect for tradition, and non-hierarchical methods of consensus building and community formation.[56]

The result of these influences is that, after giving their children the gift of a privileged education, the elder generation may be shocked when the next generation returns with radical new ideas: Why do their now-grown children not express their thanks by acceding to the traditional ways? Why do they question and want to change things? And more importantly, how can the family get them back in line?

DEMOGRAPHICS AND LONGEVITY

Demographic changes are impacting the purity of the different cultural models at an unprecedented rate. One fifteenth-generation Italian family noted to us they have seen more change in their family in the past twenty years than in the fourteen previous generations.

A related trend is the rising rate of education for women and the opening of opportunities for women in business. Daughters and wives are increasingly exposed to ideas that lead toward individualism and change. Many want to be part of a workplace culture where their newfound skills and experience can be utilized. As a result, more women are delaying or even rejecting the traditional family in favor of career, autonomy, and personal choices. Within family enterprises, they are asking for greater input and, quite literally, a seat at the table of family leadership.

Longer lives and lower birth rates are also impacting family enterprises. As the older generation achieves greater longevity, pressures to deal with change increase amid the expanding maturity and impatience of the younger generation. With family leaders retaining authority through a life expectancy of eighty or ninety years, the next generation may be in their late sixties before a transition occurs. Unlike Prince Charles of the British monarchy, they may not want to spend their whole lives in waiting.

This has major implications for family enterprises, where many families must now deal with two generational transitions in rapid sequence. The passing of a ninety-year-old patriarch or matriarch may precipitate transition in quick succession to the next leader and then to the up-and-coming third-generation designees who are already forty years old.

Young people today are also the first truly digital generation who has spent their lives with electronic connection. Millennials and Generation Xers have been exposed to elements drawn from all three of the ethnic cultures, including their own perspective. They also have a natural openness to ambicultural ideas and access to innovative solutions anywhere in the world. Their elders — raised in economically limited, non-global, non-digital worlds — find themselves struggling to understand their children and to trust their judgment.

INFORMATION FROM PEERS AND NETWORKS

In addition to family, teachers, digital media, and the classroom, young affluent individuals from successful family enterprises are learning from each other and from a wide array of social networks. Next-gens from each of the three global cultures are exposed to new ideas through the personal relationships they form and the communities they join. A twenty-something is just as likely to work and socialize alongside a peer from another culture as from their own, hearing about others' lives and families. In doing so, they also may be presented with new dilemmas about entering committed relationships with partners from halfway around the world, impacting choices back home in the family enterprise.

Immigrants and Natives in the Journey Across

Ironically, in the *Journey Across* the roles of immigrant and native are reversed, compared to the *Journey Up*. In the economic rise of the family, the founding generation makes the migration from one economic culture to another, acting as immigrants raised in one culture but arriving (and living) in a new one. Their offspring are native to the new circumstances.

In the *Journey Across*, the founding generation remains native to its ethnic heritage. They understand and accept its beliefs and its ways of behaving. The immigrants are the Next Gens who arise in the family's ethnic heritage but, like pioneers, go discover the lands that lie beyond the horizon. They in fact are often sent by the family to make this journey. The intention is that the younger generation will bring back knowledge but will somehow not be changed by their adventures. All too often, like most immigrant experiences, the journey is a life-changing experience whose impact ripples throughout the family system.

Stress Points for Families

The influences that arise in the *Journey Across* produce natural strains at predictable points for families:

WORKING TOGETHER IN THE FAMILY ENTERPRISE

The return of next-generation family members to the enterprise is a pressure point for many families. What was assumed and expected is no longer guaranteed once young people are exposed to the full range of possibilities for life in the outside world. When family members have diverse cultural experiences and perspectives, family teams may function only moderately well.

Successful families rise to this challenge and adapt. They invite sharing of ideas and innovative processes for the betterment of the enterprise. Supportive family leaders permit this influx of creativity and do not feel betrayed by it, as long as the next generation conveys ideas using as many of the communication habits of the culture as possible, maintains the established hierarchy, and demonstrates patience about the pace for change.

IN THE FAMILY DYNAMICS

The pressures of the family's *Journey Across* add to the underlying stress of their original *Journey Up*, exacerbating the sense that the generations have diverse and perhaps irreconcilable perspectives. Discord can invade parent-child relationships, pit sibling against sibling, and create damaging alliances leading to family rifts.

One brother, for example, may advocate for the parents' way of doing things, while another brother or sister may advocate for "a more modern approach" which actually represents Individualist features. The conflict then is less generational and more sibling-related, though the dangers of a major family rift are just as great. The fight may be framed not as different viewpoints or cultures but as who is the holder of the family legacy and who is "innovative" or "rebellious" (depending on one's viewpoint).

Wealth transfers are another area of vulnerability when cultures clash. Financial support, loans, gifts, and inheritances are framed very differently in the three cultures and may follow very different paths. In Honor cultures, religious influences (e.g., Sharia law) and codified traditions of inheritance (e.g., forced-heirship laws dictating fixed proportions of an estate that must go to a spouse, eldest son, or natural children) are being challenged by new Individualist-driven laws granting choice in estate planning. The rise of divorce, remarriage, and blended families adds extra layers of complexity. As new regulations are instituted permitting flexibility in the choice of estate jurisdiction, trust provisions, ownership of assets, domicile, and residency, the old mandates reinforcing authority and hierarchy are being dismantled.

An Honor Family Takes Its Feud to an Individualist Court[57]

Bal Mohinder Singh, an elderly Sikh patriarch in a prominent upscale British hotel enterprise, brought suit in the English courts to compel his son Jasminder (the head of the business) to give him a third of certain assets in the business. The patriarch asserted that the family functioned as a joint Hindu family under the Mitakshara principle of shared family wealth. He objected to Jasminder's forcing him to retire in 2010 and failing to grant him his share of property.

In emotional testimony, Bal Mohinder reportedly stated that, "as the head of the family, I have to be respected and the fact that I was forced to retire by Jasminder was very, very painful for me." He spoke of emotions and perspectives emblematic of Honor culture: "I and his mother are deeply ashamed that Jasminder should publicly renounce his cultural heritage and the mutual rights and obligations of the family system in which he was brought up... My life had been devoted to winning respect for myself and family in those communities."[58] In an example of ambiguous, high-context communication, Mr. Singh "said that the principles of a joint family are often taken for granted and are understood even if they are not being observed."[59]

Jasminder Singh, however, denied he had been brought up so deeply in Sikh religious tradition. He was educated in Christian mission schools in Kenya and finished his academic training in Britain. Nor in his view was there any such understanding of shared family wealth. He relied upon direct, written agreements and had a history of disagreeing openly with his parents in front of others, a violation of Honor principles. Despite all this, throughout the legal battle the two generations of Singhs continued to live in the same home with their families.

Expressing sympathy and understanding for the elder Singh's perspective, the British court nevertheless ruled in favor of Jasminder, the son.

IN THE FAMILY PHILANTHROPY

Family enterprises may encounter strains when attempting to implement their philanthropic endeavors across generations. Honor and Collective Harmony cultures tend to focus on their religious traditions, their heritage family connections, and their trusted networks supportive of the family tribe. Individualist families also devote themselves to these causes, but they draw from a much broader array of charitable causes and objectives less connected to family and heritage.

Cross-cultural stress can arise over grant-making, the relative balance of family donation versus branch or individual donation, the degree to which philanthropy will be unrestricted versus linked to business and outcome metrics, and other conflicts that actually have cultural roots.

East Meets West as Past Meets Future[60]

A third-generation Singaporean family business holds diverse business interests across Southeast Asia including luxury retail establishments and hotels. The family built and endowed a charitable hospital in China in the town where the first-generation founders originated.

Two fourth-generation family members who have completed their studies in the US are keen for the family and its business to have stronger philanthropic initiatives. In response, the patriarch believes they can leverage the family's commitment to the hospital in China to demonstrate the business's credentials to key stakeholders and staff. The matriarch believes the hospital should only be a family endeavor reflecting their values. She advocates that their philanthropy should not be intertwined in the business. Tension is palpable as the parents feel challenged by their children's proposals, yet they do not mention this openly. Meanwhile, the young G4 family members are not sure where to begin to establish their imprint on the family's philanthropy and the enterprise.

SUCCESSION IN THE FAMILY ENTERPRISE

Ultimately, eclipsing all other challenges, the number one strain in family enterprises in any of the three cultures occurs during generational transitions in leadership. (It is also the number one referral request by advisors for help from a family business consultant.)

Leadership transitions are difficult for several reasons. One is that succession goes smoothly only under the best of circumstances. Plus, cross-cultural family transition leaders have extra stressors to contend with. They struggle with their differing approaches to communication, trust building, leadership model, problem-solving strategy, directness, and decision-making. On top of the many differences in personal style that any leader brings to his or her position, leaders from different cultural backgrounds approach strategic planning and management with their own unique set of behaviors and beliefs. Meanwhile on the family side, the faith of the extended family in its leadership will depend on its comfort with the leader's style, clearly a function of the various cultural perspectives.

In a global environment, the enterprise must take steps to adapt to new challenges yet still preserve its identity, heritage, and relationships. This is where the elder generation leader may have strongly traditional views in conflict with a designated Next-Gen successor, threatening the success of the transition. The task is to balance continuity with adaptation in core aspects of leadership, management, and operations.

Luen Thai: Succession in a Harmony Culture Family Enterprise (continued)

With Dr. Tan as the patriarch in the Luen Thai family, the oldest son Henry in the next generation has emerged as a family leader second only to his father. Ten years ago the family decided it was time to plan actively for the future. They began a transition process that has led to shared family governance. Adapting Western ideas of governance to their own model, they created a family council, providing "structured ways to manage the family culture and values, and set policies and procedures for benefits and other family matters." They created a family office and set up three committees—education and career, health and medical, and recreation. Members of the third generation were invited to join these committees.

The family is now experiencing the active transfer by Dr. Tan to ownership and full leadership by the second generation. They are also developing the skills of G3 and inviting that generation into the business and family governance. The family is aware that the circumstance of having few women in the second generation (only one sister among five brothers) may have led women not to become involved in the business. The invitation to G3 is clearly that any family member can enter, including women.

They have become a global family, living and working in many countries, consciously blending Western ideas such as setting up a family office and crafting explicit family policies and agreements, within the traditional Chinese values of their ancestors. Their traditions are strong, but so are the values of innovation and learning from others.

Resolving the Dilemmas

The challenges facing global families on the *Journey Across* are significant. Fortunately, there is much that can be done to break impasses and resolve difficult dilemmas in service of each generation.

SECTION III

Negotiating Change Across Generations

CHAPTER 11

Negotiating the Family's Future

Families and advisors often believe that most differences within the family can be resolved by simply communicating better. Although many issues do benefit from open communication, communication alone may not be enough to manage deeply-held cultural issues.

To truly communicate and resolve issues, family members need to realize they actually are engaging in a cross-cultural negotiation. They cannot understand each other if they don't illuminate the assumptions *behind* their concerns. Only then can they understand what is driving the solutions each side is advancing. Only then can they form the agreements that lead the family out of conflict.

Unfortunately, most families have a limited sense of what healthy negotiation looks like. Negotiation may be interpreted as "hard bargaining," particularly in competitive business families: driving the best deal to win the greatest advantage. Hard bargaining is not a recipe for success when different generations or family branches with unique cultural perspectives try to achieve mutually-agreeable solutions.

Indeed, most families understand negotiation from a mindset that emphasizes power and rights: who is the strongest, who has pride of place in the family, who is entitled to have what they want, who has been most aggrieved, even who can make life most miserable for others. The natural power imbalances across generations can devolve into threats (real or potential) with family members choosing up sides for the future of the family. When trust is low or damaged and competition escalates for favored positions, negotiation can prove quite difficult.

Approaching Family Negotiations

Our orientation is based on modern negotiation methods first outlined in Fisher and Ury's classic book, *Getting to Yes*.[61] These methods have been substantially researched and expanded, to the point where much of current diplomacy and organizational negotiation is grounded in these techniques. The approach has been termed "interest-based," "integrative," or "principled" negotiation. We encourage all families and advisors to learn as much as possible about this approach and its cross-cultural variants.[62] We cannot emphasize this enough. Skillful negotiation provides a foundation for important skills that families can use whenever differences arise and conflicts must be resolved.

The basic principles of interest-based negotiation generally apply to families wishing to understand each other, move toward win-win solutions, and create outcomes that preserve relationships rather than conquer adversaries. They are a bit more challenging in practice, however, because of the complex prior relationships between family members and the emotional stakes that are often involved. Plus, family negotiations across cultures run into the same problems as cross-cultural business teams.

Take the following typical family problem based on several case anecdotes we have described:

> A patriarch from a Harmony culture wishes for his eldest son, trained and working successfully in Individualist culture, to return home and participate in the family enterprise with traditional principles. There is a second-born daughter who also has been educated and trained in the West and who currently works in the business with less recognition for her many contributions. The son is ambivalent, wishing to consider his options and hesitant to devote his life to a potentially stifling situation. Yet obeying his family and growing the family enterprise has its attractions, if certain conditions could be met.

In business, this would be seen as a classic situation for negotiation. It involves elements that are part deal-making and part dispute resolution. In this particular situation, the following factors are present:

- There is a proposal from one party to another (father to son) with stated objectives and advantages.
- The counterparty (the son) sees some advantages to accepting the

proposal. However, he also has other attractive alternatives and is hesitant to accept the proposal as is. His hesitations grow from concerns about implied or stated conditions of the proposal, e.g., leave his present job and residence to relocate, abandon career plans, and work under an authoritarian boss with limited managerial freedom for an undetermined period.

- There are interested observers who may be impacted by the outcome of the negotiation (mother, daughter/sister).
- If the conditions of the proposal can be negotiated to the satisfaction of both parties, a successful agreement may be reached and implemented. This will preserve the relationship and reduce the strains or disputes that may be developing.

The overlay of family relationships — influenced by cultural factors — is what makes this process complex and emotional. Guilt, loyalty, rejection, hurt, anger, and retaliation color the negotiation process, compared to a straightforward business transaction. Although the two parties have a close longstanding relationship, they no longer fully understand each other's recent changes and current perspectives. They may also be immersed in past injustices and assumptions, complicating their ability to focus on the issues at hand.

How, then, can families use the benefits of negotiation strategy while navigating the powerful emotional currents that often derail family communication?

KNOWING ONE'S BOTTOM LINE AND ALTERNATIVES

Before any negotiation can proceed, each party has to understand what it will and will not accept in any solution. What will you really do if you can't get your minimum requirements? What can I accept of the other person's position, and what would be unacceptable? What will the other parties do if they don't get what they want?

These represent important alternatives that will influence the course of the negotiation. In the jargon of interest-based negotiation, what you will do if you don't get your minimum requirements is called the Best Alternative to a Negotiated Agreement, or BATNA. It is what you will do if you have to walk away and leave the agreement or relationship. This is especially difficult to contemplate within a close family, who may prefer not to even think about it.

Just barely preferable to each party's BATNA lie each party's minimum requirements to stay and live with a negotiated agreement. This is each party's *bottom line*, what they are willing to accept within the negotiation at the very least.

Determining one's bottom line (if the negotiation succeeds) and BATNA (if the negotiation fails) starts with an honest and accurate appraisal of one's options. In his classic text, Albert O. Hirschman noted that when an individual or group disagrees with the established authority in an organization (or family), they have three choices:[63]

> **Loyalty:** They can stay within the system, keep silent about any objections, and remain loyal. A cost may be living with the stress of chronic internal pressure due to not voicing strongly-held differences or disagreements.
>
> **Voice:** They can stay but exercise their right of disagreement and articulate their concerns, thereby questioning or rejecting tradition and advocating for change. Possible costs include being subjected to frequent attack by an unchanging system or being marked as rebellious or disloyal.
>
> **Exit:** They can leave the system and go their own way. The payoff is freedom. But the cost may include being cast adrift from the emotional, financial, business, and even spiritual resources of the family.

These are the choices of the next generation in a family enterprise.

In our example, are all three on the table for the son? Some options such as blind loyalty or leaving the family may be undesirable, but they might still be considered if their downsides can be lessened or their benefits enhanced.

Equally important, yet even more commonly neglected, is an accurate and honest appraisal of the other party's bottom line. Does the father believe that all three options are on the table for his son? Does the father understand that his son would truly consider not joining the enterprise? Alternatively, would the son's rejection of the invitation to return be so devastating that the father would disavow and disinherit his son? Accurately assessing how far other family members will go in holding to cherished positions is something each family member must think through carefully.

Having a realistic idea of where the boundaries are for everyone clearly influences the negotiation alternatives and therefore the possible outcomes. It doesn't mean some options might not be difficult to accept. It does mean some options might be difficult and some might be truly intolerable.

A Daughter and Her Family Seek Resolution

A daughter from an Honor culture marries and goes to live in the US, where she receives her MBA and works for a large corporation. Following tradition, she leaves her family's business and becomes a member of her husband's family. Sadly, the marriage falls apart. After her divorce she asks to rejoin her family's business and return to her home country.

Her father is open to the idea of her coming back while her brothers are not. Traditionally-minded, they feel that, if their sister rejoins the business, they will be diminished in the eyes of their community. They also do not like the idea of losing some of their ownership shares and collaborating with a woman. Her father, open to her rejoining, does expect her to live in the family compound with the rest of the family.

The ensuing negotiation recognizes that the family's conflicts are rooted in differences between Honor and Individualist cultures. Through participation in a family business network, the family learns that other families are including their sister/daughters in the business and that next-generation family members often wish to live somewhat separately from the clan. The resolution is that the daughter rejoins the business, the business adopts a Code of Conduct and set of practices that reflect some Western ideas, and the daughter agrees to maintain two residences — one with the family and a weekend home in the country near her friends.

For the younger generation, there is something to keep in mind about one's bottom line. Agreeing to stay yet working internally for change may cover a significant amount of territory. A gracious offer to an authoritarian elder might be framed as, "I am happy to agree to stay and work as you wish. But will you allow me to pursue some innovative projects on my own? Can we do both?"

This "both/and" alternative reframes an "either/or" situation into a potentially multi-strategy solution. It allows for some independence while preserving loyalty, obedience, and cohesion. Particularly in Honor or Harmony cultures requiring some ambiguity in communication, it builds in significant leeway and the possibility of indirect agreement. This preserves face and lays the groundwork for future flexibility without necessarily spelling everything out. Next Gens who really do not wish to leave the family enterprise, yet are unwilling to give up all hope of future independence, may see the most possibility in agreeing to Option One (stay, with quiet loyalty and obedience) while proposing or planning for Option Two (stay, while working internally for change).

THE NEXT GENERATION AS LEGITIMATE PARTICIPANTS

In resilient families, family leaders accept that, painful as it may seem, the younger generation has power. These leaders shift from framing next-generation choice as a betrayal to understanding that Next-Gen choice is a legitimate option. The elder generation can come to hear the voices of their children not as a threat to their authority but an opportunity to learn, or at the very least, to listen. Accepting that Option Three (marked Exit) is a newly possible alternative for Next Gens is one of the most powerful consequences of family members' journey into global cultures.

Fortunately, the elder generation may be pleased to learn that the younger generation most often *wants* to remain within the family/collective and is seeking co-created solutions — in other words, negotiated agreements. When adult children engage in the process not with a sense of entitlement but with patient respect, there is opportunity for change.

WHEN THERE IS NO ROOM FOR NEGOTIATION

A reality in all three global cultures, however, is that many family members in positions of authority do not see any value in negotiating with younger and/or weaker family members. These leaders do not recognize that the prospect of losing important relationships in the family grants any power whatsoever to those willing to leave. Fulfilling one's place and destiny within the family are paramount within their cultural tradition. Independence is secondary and not to be supported. From an Individualist perspective, this is rigid authoritarianism, or closed-mindedness. From Harmony or Honor perspectives, this is leadership. It is wisdom and the voice of stability. Leaders see their role as holding and implementing authority, not delegating it.

Another variation in families with centralized authority occurs when the elder generation recognizes the need to create new governance or policies but is most comfortable doing so on behalf of the next generation, not with it. This is consistent with the paternalistic approach of those cultures.

We Are Not Yet Ready to Build Bridges between Generations[64]

A Western family business consultant worked for several years with a Harmony Culture second-generation sibling group in Southeast Asia. The siblings worked together effectively under a second generation patriarch, the eldest male. Early on, the consultant inquired about involving the third generation of the family in the process. The siblings replied, "No, let us work out the rules first. When we have decided, then we will give the constitution to the third generation for their comments. It will be too messy if we asked for their input before we know what we want." The consultant recommended incorporating into the family constitution such concepts as a separate family assembly and a forum to educate future family owners. In the final editing by the siblings, these were removed, though the family did agree to retain a council of family elders.

The constitution the siblings agreed on formalized a strong, centralized family council. However, when the time finally arrived for executing the document, the siblings decided it would ultimately be very helpful but deferred its implementation for several years. The consultant was told: "In a Western family you would involve the third generation, but our culture is different. In a Chinese family [their culture of origin] the elders decide and then tell the next generation what the rules should be." The siblings ultimately decided not to show the constitution to the third generation until later.

Although a paternalistic process may offend the sensibilities of Individualist-trained advisors or family members, it is actually an example of a hybrid approach incorporating some but not all elements of Individualism.

Much depends on the degree to which the new policies or procedures are benevolent and whether the slower pace of change can be tolerated by the next generation. If the younger generation shares the family's traditional views and is relatively passive in their acceptance of rules handed down, this solution can work. The approach is more problematic when significant numbers of the next generation are anxious to share the reins of power and have attractive outside options, often as a result of their Individualist education and training.

When elders refuse to discuss alternatives or negotiate solutions directly with the next generation, there are only a few options. One is to seek involvement from trusted third parties who may be able to explain things in terms acceptable to those in power, opening the door to negotiation (see Chapter 13 for further discussion of advisors' role in helping families). Elders may need to be guided by other family members or advisors to understand that requiring all-or-none solutions is likely to lead to damage to family members, relationships, or the family itself. Some elders have been known to listen to the friends of their grown children, sidestepping the complex feelings that arise when listening to one's own offspring.

Another option is to accept that, in this time and place, negotiation may be impossible but change may yet occur at some future date. Some families do stagnate under authoritarian leadership. But with ever-evolving conditions and people, it may be reasonable to maintain hope that change will come to the family and its enterprise. Sometimes a trusted advisor can be helpful in bringing the patriarch into contact with peers who can help loosen entrenched beliefs, though this can never be assured.

Finally, for those who do leave the family to escape intolerably closed conditions, there may yet be hope. Many who break from their family ultimately find fulfillment, recognition, or achievement within other families and enterprises. Some next-generation family leaders are welcomed elsewhere with great success. Although the loss of these great personal resources is a blow to the family of origin, it can still be a good outcome for the individual. So, exit must always be on the table in negotiations with the next generation.

Even with exit from participating in the business, family members remain connected as family and often as shareholders. In some cases, an exit from management or a board position may wind up being reversed. There are many examples of young exiles leaving, then being called back or electing to return, sometimes after they have demonstrated capability in other enterprises.

When Change May Be Possible

Assuming, then, that there is a basis for negotiation and a willingness to engage in the process, let's examine the basic steps involved in family negotiation.

CHAPTER 12

The Process of Negotiating Change

Two fundamental principles of good negotiation include a) understanding the personal issues apart from the concrete problems to be negotiated, and b) focusing on interests, not positions. Let us examine these from a family perspective.

Understanding Both the People and the Problems

Many negotiations get bogged down in the very issues central to family life. These include deeply personal matters of old history infused with assumptions and expectations rooted in relationships. The emotional factors mentioned previously — guilt, fear, anger, rejection, entitlement, hurt, envy, mistrust — pervade discussions. These factors impact each party's ability to see the main issues clearly, risking misinterpreting or mishearing what the other person is saying. These factors also complicate solutions in an attempt to fix past hurts or problems rather than just the problem(s) at hand.

Yet, trying to negotiate family matters is impossible without considering at least some of the emotions and relationship issues woven into the current dilemma. Completely "separating the people from the problem"[65] is wise in business but unrealistic in personal and family relationships. What families must do is be willing to reference the underlying emotional issues commingled with the problems at hand, either directly (as in Individualist and some Honor cultures) or obliquely (as in Harmony culture). Families must also be able to tolerate their anxiety about such discussions long enough to advance the conversation about the current crisis.

For example, in our Harmony case scenario where father and son must negotiate the son's return to the business, attempts to discuss the complex issues could easily draw in prickly allegations about assumed patterns dating back to childhood. The father might say to the son, "you always were too headstrong and disrespectful, even as a five-year-old." The son might respond with "you never let me make any choices of my own, so now I'm going to." More on point, the Individualist son may wish to voice his worry about being potentially frustrated for years in a lesser leadership position under his father than he will have with an outside company. The father (supported by the mother) may not wish to hear any of that, believing "obligation is obligation." All of this assumes, of course, that these feelings could be expressed directly to at least some degree rather than kept under the surface.[66]

Understanding both the people and the problems acknowledges emotional factors but stays focused on the dilemmas or conflicts the parties need to resolve.

The family in our case scenario might work toward framing the issues as follows:

- How can the parents be satisfied that the enterprise will continue and that the family will remain cohesive as succession passes to the next generation?
- How can the son participate in the family enterprise in a way that is personally satisfying to him?
- How can the siblings support each other as the generational transition occurs?

A cultural perspective is especially useful here in understanding both the people and the problems as a first step. Many potentially emotional landmines result from labelling behavior and assuming intentions in the other person's actions. Saying "you are only thinking of yourself" is quite personal and hurtful, framing a normal inclination toward independence as excessive selfishness. It also risks defensive retaliation with the retort, "you are being controlling, just as you always have been."

Families can step back and remember that Honor and Harmony elders see authority as natural, necessary, and appropriately traditional. Individualist Next Gens see directness as assertive, clear, and collaborative. A cultural perspective helps validate and normalize each party's viewpoints in a less judgmental way. It also keeps the focus on the issues and the process rather than relying on traditional fights over power, rights, and influence.

FOCUS ON INTERESTS, NOT POSITIONS

The core of interest-based negotiating is the fundamental distinction between interests and positions. Interests are the underlying needs or wishes that each party is trying to achieve, the bedrock of what people want. Positions are the methods, solutions, or requirements that people defend or advocate in service of achieving their interests. Interests are the destinations, positions are the roads to get there.

Confusing positions and interests is easy. Both often begin with, "I want..." and may seem to represent desired outcomes. But interests are more fundamental. They also are often more understandable than positions are.

In our example, the father may express his interest at first as, "I want you to come into the business, as is your duty." Teasing apart interest and position, however, might be more accurately articulated with, "I wish to continue our family's long, treasured legacy of son succeeding father. Your behaving as I did with my father would fulfill that." Further clarification might add, "I fear being dishonored if the legacy of family succession is broken in my generation. If you seek your future elsewhere, I would feel ashamed and lose respect in the eyes of my peers, my family, and my company." In each case, an eminently understandable interest is described first, followed by the chosen position for fulfilling that interest.

Most people form beliefs about the methods needed to achieve the outcome they want. They fight for those methods as a matter of pride, necessity, or lack of awareness of other methods. Being able to understand what the underlying goals are, combined with flexibility about the means for accomplishing those goals, can lead to new and better solutions achieved through negotiation.

Articulating what each party wants and why they want it has a side benefit. It often creates empathy and understanding in the other party, softening the process. People hesitate to reveal their underlying interests out of shame or fear of giving up a good bargaining position. But openness about interests shifts the focus from entrenched positions and creates opportunity for finding solutions. In a family, this realization can rebuild closeness around what the common interests really are. Families who are able to make their underlying interests known in an acceptable manner are much more able to reach solutions.

From a cultural standpoint, this is where communication style is crucial. In our Harmony culture example, some interests may remain unspoken or indirectly articulated with family members skilled in reading context and meaning. Loss of face may be clearly understood by everyone and unnecessary to be discussed as a likely interest.

A cross-cultural Next Gen, raised in an Honor or Harmony family but later trained in Individualist culture, may be able to take the lead in bridging the communication gap. With an insider's knowledge of family norms but newly developed skills in directness and openness, he may be able to say what his parents cannot: "I understand that our family's tradition of son succeeding father is important to you, to our family, and to our reputation. I too would prefer to see us continue that tradition and preserve our honor. If we can find ways to accommodate some concerns I have about joining the business at this time, we can probably achieve what we all want."

Successful outcomes require an understanding on everyone's part that their interests are recognized, validated, and likely to be considered in any eventual set of solutions. What is usually at issue are the methods by which interests can be fulfilled as much as possible.

TYPES OF INTERESTS

Interests come in basically three categories:

- Shared
- Conflicting or competing
- Independent, neither shared nor conflicting/competing

Common shared interests include wanting to preserve the family legacy, wanting the enterprise to thrive, wanting the family to be cohesive or harmonious, and wanting the family business to have good leadership. Shared interests are most powerful for bringing people together, since everyone is working toward a common goal. However, sharing an interest does not mean valuing it with the same priority. Family members may share an interest such as wanting the family to be cohesive, but some may prioritize this more highly than others.

Some interests are competing or conflicting enough to be incompatible, such as one person's being fully independent of the family while simultaneously being leader of the family enterprise. Another example is a family who wants to maintain traditional gender or birth-order dominance while a female or last-born family member wants to become family leader. Wanting the family to preserve its longstanding traditions and identity (by having everyone live in the family compound or be of a certain faith) is not compatible with permitting more individual choice (by allowing important family leaders to live in another region or country or adopt a different religious tradition).

Some interests are neither shared nor incompatible. Pursuing one's love of music as an avocation may be of little matter to other family members as long as responsibilities in the enterprise are fulfilled. Collective-oriented families may not care whether or how each member "feels fulfilled" in their business or personal activities as long as family obligations are met. Yet for Individualist members who learned to listen to the call of their inner passions, being able to pursue personal interests may be very important to long-term happiness within the family tribe.

As with shared interests, knowing the value or importance of competing or noncompeting interests is useful. During negotiations, the process of trading alternatives back and forth depends on trading what one holds dear and what is dispensable, much like swapping cards of lesser value to gain some of greater value in a card game. The difference is that, at its best, a successful family negotiation leaves everyone with a winning hand.

Negotiating Alternatives

The initial steps for families willing to negotiate, therefore, are to identify the personal issues to be aired, the problems to be solved, and the related interests of each party, then to determine which interests are shared, which are conflicting, and which are neither, including the relative importance each interest may have for the various parties.

With the issues, problems, and interests defined, the family can now enter a period of brainstorming and negotiating possible solutions. It is likely that at least a few elements will have to be discussed as a package deal that satisfies some interests while conceding on others. Some interests or positions may have to get dropped altogether, while others will percolate to the top as crucial for one or both sides. This is where learning to hear what is most important to the other party and what can be conceded is necessary for everyone. It is also where trade-offs can occur, either as individual elements or package deals, drawn from the priorities of each party.

It is helpful to be able to put options on the table for a period of time without evaluating their suitability in the ultimate agreement. All options have pros and cons; none is perfect. Being able to make a proposal for discussion is more valuable than having each proposal accepted or discarded as it stands. Finding ways to make alternatives work is more productive than attacking or defending the proposal.

In some families, contributions from siblings or other family members at the table can move the process forward. These stakeholders may be able to articulate perspectives or advocate for alternatives in ways that unlock value for all parties. This may also be consistent with the collective orientation of the family, compared to a more one-on-one approach.

An iterative process of proposing alternatives, listening to the other side, fine-tuning options, and benchmarking the potential result against shared interests is the essence of good negotiating for families.

For our family example, the following list could result from identifying the core problems to be resolved:

1. The family needs to maintain cohesion and harmony, long-term, with respect of the patriarch
2. The family business needs an additional executive in the management team who understands strategy
3. The family business needs a succession plan
4. Due to health issues with the parents and industry trends, a transition plan needs to occur within the next five years
5. The next generation needs to have work that is fulfilling, offers

advancement, and permits a certain level of autonomy and recognition (desired by the next generation more than by the elder generation)

6. The family needs to preserve its reputation within its community, clan, and business relationships as it undergoes transition

Table 12-1 summarizes the various interests of each family member:

Interests:	Shared	Competing	Neither Shared Nor Competing
Father	Keep family in the business, maintain authority in the family	Preserve tradition by passing business to son	Continue business success by growing business in new, diversified ways
Mother	Maintain family harmony and cohesion, uphold father's authority	Support husband and tradition while supporting son and daughter	Fulfill lifelong interest in learning new cooking skills by going to culinary school
Son	Preserve family relationships, support father's authority	Achieve success by working in another industry (no interest in family business)	Achieve personal happiness by marrying a Westerner, maintaining a home in the West
Daughter	Support the family enterprise including father's authority	Achieve success by taking leadership position in family business	Achieve personal happiness by pursuing interests in information technology

Table 12-1: List of interests for family negotiation example

USING VALUES TO CLARIFY INTERESTS AND PRIORITIES

One useful technique for sorting through solutions is to focus on the values of the family, individually and collectively. Values are the beacons, the spiritual and moral compasses that guide behavior and keep actions on track. There are several values exercises available that help families learn what they hold in common and what they differ in, such as the Values Edge cards developed by one of us (Dennis Jaffe).[67] An exercise like this can be very productive in clarifying why family members act and believe the way they do.

The values-sharing begins with each individual defining their 15 most important values, sorted into rows using cards forming a pyramid. In the ensuing discussion, family members in each generation can literally see how their values reflect different personal and cultural styles.

Similar to identifying interests, identifying values helps family members articulate what is most important to them, why, and at what priority level. Seeing others' values distilled and sorted by priority can help pinpoint that a value is shared but not rated as highly as someone else feels. After exploring individual values and differences, the family can then recognize values they share as a family. This may be their first opportunity to negotiate a balance or fusion of values. By talking about values first, they embark on the path to working through their differences with greater understanding.

In our Harmony case scenario, the family may discover through a values exercise just how much the different cultural traditions of each generation are impacting their perspectives. The parents are likely to endorse values of family, tradition, loyalty, trust, and harmony. The son and daughter undoubtedly will choose some of those cards as well, which would please the parents. Higher in priority, however, may be values of personal growth, courage, self-knowledge, achievement, and seeking challenges. Seeing this may allow the father in particular to grasp how much each of his children has been changed by their education and experiences, much more than he anticipated.

Cultural Negotiation Styles

Cross-cultural negotiation between generations can be difficult due to the communication, trust, and problem-solving approaches of each cultural style. Harmony, Honor and Individualist cultures negotiate in very different ways along the dimensions outlined in Chapter 2:

- The level of emotional expression, transparency, and direct communication during negotiations.

  Each culture tolerates a different level of emotionality and directness during negotiations. Individualist cultures prize keeping one's head, staying logical and reasonable, and avoiding excessive displays of anger or frustration.

Harmony negotiators may hide emotions behind a placid exterior or may consciously use angry or indignant outbursts as negotiating ploys to gain the upper hand. Honor cultures may be more emotionally dramatic, particularly when feeling (or wishing to emphasize) being dishonored or insulted by proposals. It is easy to misunderstand the behaviors of other cultures at the negotiating table, leading to breakdowns in communication or the negotiation itself.

- Negotiating the agreement as a whole with interrelated elements versus discussion of individual points one-by-one.

Individualist cultures like to go through point-by-point, while in Harmony (and some Honor) cultures the various elements may be viewed in context and negotiated as a package. Harmony cultures especially are good at understanding nuance, complexity, and context in other domains, such as in business. They may need to make this connection to family dilemmas. Negotiating agreements as a whole with a certain level of ambiguity allows family leaders to accept the voice of the next generation without feeling an intolerable loss of their traditional authority or "face." Harmony cultures also are able to tolerate apparent contradictions more easily than Individualist cultures, for example.

- Level of clarity of individual elements or entire agreements.

There may be an emphasis on specific behaviors and action steps (e.g., someone will be appointed chief operating office within two years) or on abstract principles or concepts (e.g., respect and loyalty will be granted at all times to family leaders). Families with members of various cultures under one roof will have to find a balance between explicitness and ambiguity in negotiated agreements, while not skirting areas of difference simply to avoid conflict.

- The use of third parties during negotiation versus direct communication within the family.

In Individualist culture, direct negotiations are assumed to be best. This is consistent with the values of self-sufficiency, individual responsibility, assertiveness, and avoidance of drawing outsiders into internal family matters (not "triangulating" others into a relationship). Harmony or Honor cultures see the use of third-party elders and trusted advisors as helpful involvement from the collective family system. The use of third parties may serve to keep the level of direct conflict manageable while agreements are being constructed.

- How trust is reinforced, rebuilt, or verified later during implementation of the agreement.

  Repairing or rebuilding of trust may be important results of new agreements within families, particularly if there has been significant conflict before or during negotiations. Demonstrating trust between family members may be linked to performance or completion of specific tasks within defined timelines, or it may be reinforced through relationship-building, loyalty, and proving of allegiance over long periods of time.

For our family example, we might imagine that the following multipart solution could be achieved through the course of discussion and negotiation:

- After being allowed to voice some important emotional issues in respectful terms, the son agrees to return home for a period of five years and take a management position in order to facilitate the planning and transition process. He concedes this has important strategic value to the family enterprise in the eyes of customers, professional relationships, and his parents, which he is willing to support.
- The father agrees that if, after four years, the son still wants to work elsewhere, the father will support that and work toward finding other family or nonfamily executives for the position.
- The family agrees to consider placing both the son and the daughter on the board of the business. The son also agrees to continue serving on the board even if he eventually leaves management in the operating company.

- The son and daughter persuade their parents that having a female family executive has great value in today's global market. With the daughter's skills, her interest in the business, and the new opportunity to tout gender diversity as an enterprise value, the father sees he may be able to achieve his hope for family succession if he shifts his focus to his daughter from his son. The planned five-year transition period with his son in the business makes the hand-off more palatable and likely to succeed. The relationship between the siblings also deepens as a result of their supporting each other's interests.

- The daughter and father find common ground in anticipating new business ventures using information technology.

- The mother helps facilitate discussion at difficult points in the process. She is very happy with the outcome since it fulfills her hopes that no major rifts will split the family.

- The son feels exceptional relief in having his concerns heard and acknowledged by his father. As a result, he is much more willing to accept a disruption in his life plans. The door remains open to pursue his real professional interests outside the family business. He is able to fulfill his family obligations as a respected member, yet he is granted the independence that is important to him.

Points to Consider

By using interest-based negotiation with a cross-cultural perspective, families can make great progress along their journeys to success. Nevertheless, negotiation across branches, generations, and cultures may be one of the hardest challenges for a family enterprise. Here are some helpful points for families working through agreements:

TACKLE TOUGH ISSUES WITH PATIENCE AND ENGAGEMENT

Negotiating requires patience and toleration of conflict without anticipating the family will be destroyed. Although this is especially difficult in Harmony and Honor cultures, many Individualist families are just as afraid of open conflict. Sometimes those in positions of power or authority in a family shut down the discussion out of fear of the strong feelings or perspectives that are expressed. They are not necessarily being controlling; they are simply unable to tolerate open family tension. Persevering through tough conversations requires the family to debate differences without anyone short-circuiting the process.

SEEK RESOURCES

Attending family business conferences and reading the many articles and books available on family business may broaden perspectives and help validate the cross-cultural arguments being made across the table.

DON'T GO IT ALONE

Outside parties may be invaluable for successful outcomes. Third parties can help calm the process and provide emotional stability to angry, discouraged, or exhausted participants losing stamina. The next chapter examines the unique role of advisors for helping client families persevere through the sometimes arduous process of understanding each other and negotiating change.

CHAPTER 13

The Advisor as Cultural Mediator

Standing alongside every global family enterprise are many advisors: private bankers, attorneys, accountants, wealth managers, family office executives, family business consultants, and others. Some of these advisors may have accompanied the family for years during the *Journey Up*, others in the *Journey Across*. Some advisors are more recent arrivals into the family's life, as the family is trying to cope with the complex world in which it now finds itself.

Increasingly, advisors need to develop competencies about cultural differences and how to offer advice that acknowledges cultural factors when working with ambicultural families. There are several fundamental issues that advisors must become aware of in advising global family enterprises, with practical recommendations for applying this knowledge in service for their clients.

Know Thyself

First, advisors must be aware of the personal cultural lens they bring to their work with clients of various cultures and how their advice may be influenced by assumptions that reflect a specific cultural bias. This is especially important when the advisor's client base is predominantly from one culture, and that culture is the advisor's own heritage. That is where blind spots may occur most frequently.

We have discussed elsewhere[68] about the *Journey Up,* the "Immigrants and Natives" metaphor, and how advisors need to examine their own biases and stereotypes when working with client families. There are advisors who find themselves resenting the privileges of wealth or inheritance, or who are dismissive of in-laws or the initiatives of the younger generation. Others resent the power and authority of the wealth-creating generation or blindly support anything their "primary client" desires. Many of these biases grow from the advisor's own economic background and station in life, transferred to the advising relationship.

Similarly, many professional advisors have been raised and professionally educated within one cultural model, whether that is Harmony, Honor, or Individualist culture. This will affect how they see their clients, what they may think is natural, and what they may think is strange.

Sharing a cultural heritage with a client will certainly foster understanding and help develop rapport. A risk, however, is that the advisor will also share the client's perspectives on exactly those issues that are creating conflict or impasses across generations. An example is aligning with an Honor or Harmony patriarch that their authority needs to be asserted and reinforced, rather than seeing the validity of fresh perspectives from an Individualist Next Gen. Or, advocating for an Individualist family branch that is pushing for directness, egalitarianism, and transparency, without respecting the elders' long traditional history of approaching change slowly and preserving harmony along the way.

The more that advisors undertake learning about how cultures differ, how these factors present in the advising relationship, and especially how families function in various cultures, the better-prepared they will be to recognize their biases and respond less judgmentally.

Searching for a Solution in a Difficult Situation

A family of Middle-Eastern origin, living in the US, appeared to their advisory team to be having significant family dynamics problems. The ways of the Honor culture in the elder generation conflicted with those of some family members (and several advisors) in Individualist America. Many consultants were invited by the adult members of the next generation to help the family, but their ideas about shared governance and transparency ran into a wall from the patriarch. The patriarch adhered strongly to Honor procedures, shooting down change and trying to enforce traditional ways even in the family's adoptive land. He used indirect communication, did not trust the integrity of the advisors, threatened to veto any change until he is dead, and vowed to cast off any of his children who do not comply with his wishes. The alliance of younger family members and US advisors got nowhere.

Finally, one advisor helped the patriarch meet other elders who were better able to listen to their grown children. The advisor and a few of the outside elders brought the patriarch to some family business conferences that began to stretch his perspective. Now, the patriarch had a new reference group of successful family business founders whom he could confide in, listen to, and model himself after. He began to be more open to the ideas of his children.

Cultural Intelligence in the Advising Relationship

Advisors must be culturally sensitive when engaging with a family from a culture other than their own. Acting in a culturally incongruent manner can lead to failure of the advising relationship, sometimes without the client family's being open about what went wrong.

There are many large and small behaviors and norms that differ from one culture to another, such as forms of address, who should be at meetings, where people should sit, how tasks will be defined, and how payment or work arrangements will be handled. Advisors working with traditional Asian Next Gens, for example, need to create openings for those Next Gens to speak up, since well-mannered Asians will wait politely to give opinions or ask questions in a group or family meeting. Young Individualist family members will assertively inject themselves in conversations. Advisors who keep talking and do not stop to make room for Harmony culture members might assume more agreement or acquiescence in the room than really exists.

Building trust with the key people in the family, for example, must be accomplished in a culturally-congruent manner. With some, it may be a straightforward process of acting in a reliable, responsive way on assigned tasks. With others, there may be a long process of getting to know each other before any real business is conducted.

The use of a *cultural coach* offers the advisor a way to approach cross-cultural issues before attempting to assist the client family in those delicate matters that are creating stress.

Eyes Opened to the Role of Culture: One Consultant's Story[69] (Dennis Jaffe)

Twenty years ago, when I was first approached by the third-generation son of a large Indian family, I had no cross-cultural experience. My answer to whether I understood Hindu culture was to suggest that the dynamics of family enterprise, across generations and in the creation of boundaries and agreements between business and family, were universal. This was partly true, in that family enterprises all over the world have some similar family dynamics. But I was unaware of important cultural features affecting this family.

Following the Honor model, this family structure placed the family first, with the father's authority paramount. The whole family owned all assets in common and lived together in a family compound. With each one having responsibility for different businesses, rivalry and competition were rampant, leading to high levels of conflict and few methods to resolve them other than by edict from the father. It was difficult to have the family adhere to agreements made in family meetings.

I asked to be assigned a "culture coach" to educate myself in the issues facing the "Hindu undivided family" culture and tradition. This person would be available to me when I was working with the family. Coaching allowed me to slowly understand how much the family was the core reality and that it was not easily questioned. I learned about cultural traditions of strict family equality in relation to money and work, arranged marriage with its emphasis on obligations to the whole family, secrecy about business and finances, living together in a family compound, and women's limited role in business but indirect power within the family.

A Western consultation model would have recommended for the brothers in conflict to separate their businesses and operate with more autonomy. But Hindu tradition meant that they were to receive equal salaries and benefits from their work. Traditional Western ideas of accountability and explicitness were contradicted by the Honor ideal of remaining in one's established position in the hierarchy when loyal to the leader.

Looking back, it is easy to see how this consultation, even with the presence of a cultural coach, ran aground on the culture gap between consultant and family.

The expanding recognition of cross-cultural factors in global business means that most major cities have academic or business centers with experts in cross-cultural norms, beliefs, and behaviors, such as the executive education programs at INSEAD (www.insead.edu) or IMD (www.imd.org/executive-education). Global consulting practices and organizations such as the Family Firm Institute (www.ffi.org) and STEP (www.step.org — formerly the Society of Trust and Estate Practitioners) also offer programs and consultants who can provide coaching on cultural issues in family enterprises.

Disclosing the use of a cultural coach may have a side benefit when carefully shared with a client. The advisor who models cultural intelligence by pointing out instances of cross-cultural diversity can sensitize family members to doing the same. It may lead the family to realize they too require increased awareness and skill in communicating together, perhaps through the services of the advisor or a consultant.

HELPING FAMILIES CONSIDER CULTURE

In the normal course of the advising relationship, advisors have opportunities to help educate or "stretch" family members to understand the role of culture in the many areas outlined in this book. A few examples:

- Patriarchs (and matriarchs) from all cultures can be assisted to see that benevolent intentions to manage everything for the family can be moderated by creating an educated and capable next generation.
- A leader from an Honor or Harmony culture, wanting to hold his options close to the vest and not share information with other family members, might be persuaded that limited sharing and discussion with the next generation can useful under controlled conditions. The advisor may be in a unique position to reassure the patriarch that, with appropriate safeguards, sharing selected

information will not threaten his traditional authority or the security of the family. Negotiating what those safeguards might be could be a path towards broader discussions later.

- When advising younger generations frustrated with the pace or direction of change, advisors can help explain that their ideas arise from their cultural education and experience. Finding ways to bridge their proposed changes with the heritage culture of their family will require negotiation that may take time and patience.

Using tactful, diplomatic language and a cross-cultural framework, advisors can point out advantages to at least considering some level of collaboration and negotiation.

A Conflict of Cultures[70]

An emotionally difficult situation arose when the three children in an Honor family, living in the West, were presented with the request from their traditional-minded patriarch to marry someone acceptable to him, i.e., someone from their Muslim faith. To these Individualist-educated children, the request felt unacceptable. "We will choose our own spouses," was their response. To the father, this meant they risked being disinherited.

While the children were prepared to be cast out of the family, they retained hope that further discussion would lead to a better outcome. The father was helped by advisors to understand that living in the West and having a Western education would naturally create certain consequences for the family. The younger generation stood their ground but were guided to do so with respect and concern for their parents. They were able to voice their desire to live according to their own personal integrity and yet remain deeply connected to their parents and their heritage. The family continues the delicate process of negotiating their unique mixture of tradition and adaptation.

BE FLEXIBLE ABOUT FAMILY LEADERSHIP TRAITS AND MODELS

Families undergoing succession in the family enterprise are under particular stress, especially around definitions of effective leadership in next-generation leaders. A trusted family advisor may be asked to assess the capabilities of the next generation for taking over the family business, surveying such qualities as initiative, drive, responsibility, or maturity.

Interestingly, assessment research shows that what one culture considers "drive" may be very different in another culture:

> No country in the world denies there's a preference for driven leaders. Drive, and its many vague definitions, can seem to some countries (like the US, Germany and Australia) as unfettered self-initiation and a proactive method of taking charge based on strivings for power, status and reward anticipation. Accordingly, those who decide first and rally followership later tend to appear more leader-like to their colleagues. However, in more consensus-driven societies such behaviors rarely rise through the ranks. Rather, in places like Mainland China, Japan and South Korea, those considered leaders tend to focus more on being dependable, self-disciplined and achievement-oriented; in these locations those who generate alignment first and then push forward are more likely to have the leadership label ascribed to them.[71]

The advisor can be the first one to identify that a Next-Gen leader, trained in Individualist culture but returning to an Honor or Harmony enterprise, is being rejected or mislabeled due to cultural misunderstanding of leadership skills. Advisors can help families get outside evaluations from established leadership development programs to resolve elders' concerns about their young successors. Professional programs can also be used to mentor family successors and help the family recognize competency for the global environment.

Advisors can also be extremely helpful in providing white papers, reading resources, outside speakers, and client forums that demonstrate a broader range of governance and leadership models for families to consider. Rather than proffer these to all cultures as best practices, these should be framed as useful alternatives for families to consider and adapt. The pros and cons of various governance models can be discussed in a culturally-sensitive manner to broaden their perspectives. This allows families to evaluate for themselves what is helpful *and* what seems possible.

ASSISTING WITH CROSS-CULTURAL NEGOTIATION

Above all, capable advisors can provide much-needed assistance when families become stuck in cross-cultural generational conflicts. Many advisors use negotiation skills in the normal course of their work with clients, organizations, businesses, and colleagues. The advisors clients turn to the most for help with their family enterprises — attorneys, private bankers, accountants, even some trustees — are often in a good position to help clients if they have the skills to do so.

Two specific tips may help with family negotiations:

- Serving as an intermediary with the next generation or hosting the meetings where discussions occur may be a very useful step forward for a family paralyzed by the conflict. Advisors may have to hold conversations with members of each generation or branch before they come together to discuss their differences. This is known to be useful in dispute resolutions when the emotional tension may be too high to initiate direct meetings between the parties. A bit of shuttle diplomacy may get negotiations started so family members can later sit down together productively and work on alternatives.

- Negotiating parties often expect their opposite numbers to behave using the same tactics as they do.[72] People are often unprepared to handle counterparties who have markedly different approaches, leading to frustration, irritation, giving in too early, or leaving the negotiation altogether. Elders rooted in the family's heritage culture may use their traditional methods of negotiating, while Individualist-trained Next Gens may expect to hammer out agreements like they do with peers or their Western colleagues. An advisor with ambicultural experience (or access to a skilled colleague) may be able to bridge the techniques or at least explain the differences to each family member.

We recognize that poorly-trained advisors in any culture can make negotiations worse rather than better. Advisors can make errors in aligning or advocating inappropriately with one side, distorting messages or motivations, or even skewing the outcome for their own purposes. We also recognize that Individualist-trained family business consultants may believe that any advisor involvement in family conflicts is inappropriate. They view this as getting enmeshed in what should remain direct communication between family members.

The reality is that, in many cultures, using close family advisors or trusted members of a clan or community is a natural strategy for resolving family conflicts. The important factor is for that advisor to act responsibly, ethically, and skillfully in service of his or her client.

Only a small minority of advisors is trained in the advanced interest-based negotiation techniques that work best with families, however. All advisors working with family enterprises need to educate themselves in these techniques to a proficient level. In addition to reading resources, there are educational programs and online materials from the Harvard Law School Program on Negotiation (www.pon.harvard.edu) which provide extensive training and role-playing scenarios for learning cross-cultural negotiation.

These skills build technical acumen as well as emotional strengths for assisting families working through their differences. More heat than light gets generated in families trying to negotiate deeply-held issues touching on heritage, tradition, parent-child relationships, family roles, and future contingencies. A seasoned, calm advisor who helps clients persevere to a successful agreement not only preserves family bonds but helps avoid costly litigation and potentially the breakup of a prosperous family enterprise.

RISKS TO CONSIDER

The role of intermediary in family negotiations is not an easy one. It does have its risks which need to be carefully considered.

Many advisors are wary of getting involved in emotionally-heated discussions in any culture. This is especially true in Honor or Harmony cultures where the family leader may be closed to voices advocating compromise or negotiation. Those leaders may want only an advocate, not a coach or mediator. The client relationship may be threatened by a vindictive client who wants no disagreement from anyone.

Trusted advisors with a well-established relationship may feel a bit braver in offering new perspectives for leaders to consider. Yet realistically, many advisors don't wish to risk alienating their main client. For those situations, referral to a well-credentialed outside consultant may feel like a more prudent course of action.

At the same time, advisors need to keep in mind the next generation has legitimacy and is watching closely. Ample research demonstrates that, with the death of the patriarch or matriarch, the younger generation seeks their own advisors in the majority of cases. Advisors who always align with their first-generation wealth creator, never providing even reasonable support for legitimate alternative perspectives, should expect to find those client assets going out the door when transition occurs to the new leaders. Taking the expedient route of never challenging the current client may ultimately result in losing the client account later.

A more balanced approach is to act as the next generation is advised to behave: be respectful and deferential, but find opportunities to propose progressive ideas that help the family adapt over time. Showing the next generation that their input is being heard and considered has long-term benefits that should be kept in mind. It's also the right thing to do. Offer to help negotiate when it seems reasonable to do so, and seek out others who may be in a position to offer advice and support to both sides in the conflict.

Helping the Family on the Road to Adaptation

Advisors working with global families bear new responsibilities to understand the role of culture in family dynamics. By educating themselves in ambicultural concepts and techniques, they can avoid getting their advice caught within cultural conflicts that lead the family to reject their wisdom or their services.

A family's advisors may in fact be in the best position to offer solutions, emotional support, outside resources, and generally wise perspective when the generations struggle to reach understanding. This may be one of the most helpful roles an advisor can fulfill.

CHAPTER 14

Thriving in the Global Landscape

Success in the founding generation of a prosperous enterprise leads families to a new cultural reality on many levels. They enter a broader world beyond their culture of origin, where novel, sometimes contradictory values, traditions, rules, and practices are common. We have presented a new model to explain what families encounter and to propose pathways for successfully navigating this unfamiliar cultural territory.

Cross-cultural psychology teaches that integration of old and new tends to be best when dealing with new circumstances.[73] Integration preserves core identity and values while permitting necessary adaptation. Families who work together to integrate their cultural perspectives create a healthy balance of Independence and Interdependence that accomplishes the following:

- The creation of identity best-prepared for the modern global world, integrating solid individual self-esteem with deeply-connected family identity.
- The broadest mix of skills for family members, preparing people for wealth and success across generations.
- Individual achievement without having to leave the family.
- Both strong leadership and skillful collaboration, depending on the family's unique blend of governance.
- Support for capable new leaders while insuring checks and balances on leadership.
- Passing on the values of the family to support success across generations.

As families make the *Journey Up* and the *Journey Across* in the modern world, they can enrich themselves and their legacies by incorporating perspectives from other cultures, restoring confidence as they resolve unanticipated challenges.

A Global Extended Family Looks to the Future (Part 4 of 4)

Simón Borrego and Vanessa Wen Borrego remained connected to two large extended families. They raised two daughters and a son who reflected the family's global cultural heritage. Typical for both Asian and Latin families, they sent their children off to attend a US preparatory school known for its international student body.

New challenges arose in the third generation as their children grew up surrounded by affluence, international travel, prestigious schools, and multicultural friends. Their three children, like the children of Simón's siblings and cousins and those of Vanessa's sister Lisa, were highly Westernized. They were direct, emotionally expressive communicators with notions of equality, democracy, and the justice of established governments. Yet they also had a ready familiarity with multiple countries and customs beyond that of their parents and grandparents. They could seem chameleon-like in their ability to navigate different environments. They spoke Mandarin and a bit of Cantonese along with fluent English and Spanish. They also seemed least connected to their Spanish and Chinese roots, compared to their parents.

As Wen Ho retired and Juan Borrego passed away from a heart attack, Simón and Vanessa's now-adult children participated more actively in their family's businesses and governance. They advocated for opportunities in the Asian family business as well as in Spain in the Borrego enterprise. The Wen and Borrego families began to pool their expertise and financing to pursue ventures in Miami, Vancouver, Dubai, and Eastern Europe. With the support of the family, one of the Wen Family granddaughters chose to work with nongovernmental organizations (NGOs) on social development projects in developing countries.

What began as one modest clothing factory in rural China and a manufacturing enterprise in Spain eventually blossomed into a real estate, textile, and financial conglomerate. Over three generations, two families, succeeding in their own countries, became global, with children in the second and the third generation seeing a greater range of opportunities and possibilities. Wen Ho's choice to take in Simón, and Simón's breakaway choice of a family enterprise not from his own bloodline, proved challenging but ultimately rewarding for the entire extended family.

Opportunities for Research

With the cultural model of wealth extending now across global cultures, exciting new avenues open up for research. A few ideas to consider:

- Clarifying the three cultures in family enterprises:

  Family business academic and research centers can and should begin to study the applicability of the cross-cultural model with family enterprises around the world. There is much to be analyzed, such as measures of the various cultural dimensions (trust, problem-solving style, balance of individual versus family orientation, etc.) and their correlation to variables of success in families and their businesses. Researchers can cross-pollinate their findings with the new studies coming out of management schools and international business programs on the three global cultures.

- Reanalyzing research findings through an ambicultural lens:

  Many family business research studies originate in specific cultural traditions, with differing results. Researchers may take a fresh look at interpreting their findings using a cross-cultural perspective based on the emerging data on the three global cultures.

- Clarifying the nature of the ambicultural blend and its relationship to successful families:

  Research can explore comparisons of global high-net-worth (under $30 Million US dollars [USD]) and ultra-high-net-worth families (over $30 Million USD) to look at family cultural styles. It would be interesting to verify how much families do shift in cultural style from their ethnic culture of origin to a more blended, fusion-type of family culture, with any correlation to success across generations.

- Clarifying the role of having operating companies within the family enterprise versus having primarily family wealth:

    A useful research comparison would involve analyzing ambicultural families that continue to have one or more operating companies versus those who have transitioned to becoming primarily wealth-owning enterprises.

- Fine-tuning techniques for cross-cultural negotiation in families:

    There are multiple opportunities to study cross-cultural negotiation techniques in Individualist, Harmony, and Honor cultures to see similarities and differences compared to cross-cultural business teams with nonfamily (nonrelated) members.

Family business consulting can, in general, begin to explore more culturally-aware techniques for helping families and family enterprises, less anchored to Individualist principles and perspectives. We encourage families to collaborate with their advisors and consultants on more hybrid and fusion models for adapting to the cultural stresses they experience.

Making New Choices in an Honor Culture Family

A male second-generation leader in a Greek family was being groomed for succession in the family business. His father and his father's advisors informed him that the family policy was to keep the other family shareholders in the dark, that there was no need for him to share any information with them.

The G2 successor had a brother and two sisters who each had been given 25% of the available ownership shares. He responded to his father that there was no way he could or would keep relevant information from his siblings. He also felt connected to his sisters' husbands who wanted to know what was happening in the enterprise.

Persevering through the family conflict, the next-generation family leader began sharing information that eventually led to a well-functioning family council and dramatic growth of the family enterprise.

The Outcomes in Cross-Cultural Adaptation

The end result of respectful engagement across generations is that different cultural and economic perspectives can become balanced and blended. Several steps take place as a family creates a blended family culture across generations:

- **Engage and Share:** As family members learn, work, and live in diverse places far from the family's origins, each generation shows active interest about what is being learned and how the lessons can be used by the family. Families find the time and opportunity to share these experiences, and each family member is seen as a resource who can contribute to the family.
- **Listen and Learn:** In regular exchanges, each person is able to step outside his or her usual viewpoint to learn that the family can try new activities and engage in new solutions. Learning flows both ways, not just from the older to the younger generations. Cultural intelligence allows families to appreciate, learn from, and blend the best elements of each cultural style.
- **Experiment and Blend:** The ability to adapt grows as a result of the willingness to try fresh alternatives. The family learns to experiment with new initiatives, with oversight by more experienced family members and a sense of collaboration about the outcome.

Fulfilling the Family's Destiny

As character is destiny for the individual, culture is destiny for the family. By treating generational issues as partly cultural, families are able to frame issues and negotiate solutions in highly adaptive ways. They then can navigate the challenges of an increasingly global world.

APPENDIX

Basics of Family Governance

FAMILY GOVERNANCE REFERS TO POLICIES AND PRACTICES THAT ORGAnize how a family shares information, makes decisions, and manages its members fairly. At its best, it balances the divergent needs of the family as a whole, its individual members, and the family's business and financial affairs.

Typically, in the first generation of wealth creation or business formation, the founders decide the mission, policies, and practices of the family. This is usually done informally and without sharing much information with other family members. As the family grows in size and complexity across generations, its centralized informal operating principles must be adapted to new realities. Family members benefit from becoming more structured and explicit in how they express their values, formulate policies, and make decisions. Doing this reduces the conflicts that can arise when individuals within the family are unclear about rules or expectations about money and power.

Prosperous families often also have numerous legal, financial, and business agreements that impact the lives of family members. It is useful to have a forum where the family can discuss how these agreements fit together and to reconcile differing agreements or dilemmas.

Two Fundamental Tools of Governance

Every culture has a history of having prominent families whose internal leadership governed the family and its interests wisely. In the modern world, these best practices have been codified and developed so any family can function well and care for its members.

Two tools are commonly used by successful families, more commonly in Individualist culture but evident in all cultures:

FAMILY COUNCIL

A *family council* is a group of family members who meet, discuss, share information, and make decisions for the family's benefit. It is the vehicle by which family governance is implemented. The council guides the family in areas such as shared family activities, development of the next generation, management of the family's relationship to its enterprises, and resolution of internal disagreements.

Family councils help identify and articulate the family's mission, values, and long-term legacy. They also formulate policies such as who can be on the council, how any voting may occur, when leaders are elected or appointed, how programs like financial education may be developed, and other matters. Good policies are not just wise. They also are written in clear language everyone can understand and convey a sense of justice to family members.

In a small family, depending on the family's culture, the council may include all adult family members or may limit membership to a subset, such as only males or bloodline members. In larger families, the council often is a smaller representative group drawn from various constituencies such as family branches, generations, business shareholders, or trust beneficiaries.

A family council is different from a board of directors for the family's operating company. The council is a parallel entity that exists alongside the board, doing the "business" of the family, just as the board of directors sets policy and takes care of the enterprises the family owns or operates.

A council usually meets on a regular basis, soliciting input from and communicating its decisions back to the family. The entire family may also meet from time to time in a *family assembly*. At family assemblies, the family council may listen to the views or needs of the broader family and update the family on important events, information, or decisions.

FAMILY CONSTITUTION

The *family constitution* is a written family agreement that sets down the rules, procedures, and operations of the family and how the family interacts with its businesses, if any. It outlines the governance activities that everyone is expected to adhere to.

A family constitution is a working document that guides the family in its regular interactions with each other, its assets, and its responsibilities. It can be amended and updated according to a process outlined in one of its own policies. It is usually not a legal agreement, though it is often drafted to clarify the agreements that lie in the family's legal, trust, and corporate agreements. Sometimes aspects of legal agreements which are implicit or unclear are more clearly described in the family constitution.

A family constitution is typically a signed agreement that is morally binding on family members. It helps define expectations, principles, procedures, and decision-making processes that regulate the activities the family pursues together. When created thoughtfully, a family constitution is an intergenerational agreement which hopefully will be supported by emerging new generations of the family.

For further information on family governance, please see the following:

Dennis T. Jaffe, *Stewardship in Your Family Enterprise: Developing Responsible Family Leadership Across Generations* (Changeworks, 2010).

Angelo Robles, James Grubman, and Dennis T. Jaffe, *Guiding Governance: Clarifying the Practice of Family Enterprise Governance* (Family Office Association, 2013). Available at the authors' websites (www.familyofficeassociation.com, www.jamesgrubman.com, www.dennisjaffe.com)

Notes

1. Jeanne M. Brett, *Negotiating Globally: How to Negotiate Deals, Resolve Disputes, and Make Decisions Across Cultural Boundaries, 3rd Edition* (San Francisco: Jossey Bass, 2014), 25.
2. This quotation and its associated description are adapted from the unpublished research archives on long-term global families undertaken by Dennis Jaffe at Wise Counsel Research Associates. Throughout this book, excerpts of selected interviews are described with identifying information altered to protect the privacy and confidentiality of the families involved. Where family information is either in the public domain or has been published elsewhere with permission of the family, names and identifying information are retained.
3. The term "ambicultural" is emerging in the literature from several directions, coined by various researchers and commentators. For examples, see Ming-Jer Chen and Danny Miller, "West Meets East: Toward an Ambicultural Approach to Management," *Academy of Management Perspectives* 24:4 (2010), 17–24; and, LatinWorks, *The Plus Identity: Shifting Paradigms and the Future of Latino Culture in the U.S.* (2013).
4. The names and details of this extended case anecdote are a fictionalized version of several families' histories.
5. Edwin T. Hall, *Beyond Culture* (Anchor Books, 1977).
6. Hyejeong Chung and Jerry Gale, "Family Functioning and Self-Differentiation: A Cross-Cultural Examination," *Contemporary Family Therapy* 31 (2009), 21.
7. Geert Hofstede, *Culture's Consequences* (Sage Publications, Inc., 1980).
8. Charles Hampden-Turner and Fons Trompenaars, *Building Cross-Cultural Competence* (New Haven: Yale University Press, 2000); Erin Meyer, *The Culture Map: Breaking Through the Invisible Boundaries of Global Business* (Philadelphia: Public Affairs, 2014).
9. Michele J. Gelfand, Jana L. Raver, Lisa Nishii, Lisa M. Leslie, Janetta Lun, Beng Chong Lim, Lili Duan, Assaf Almaliach, et al., "Differences between Tight and Loose Cultures: A 33-Nation Study." *Science* 332 (2011), 1100–1104; J. Douglas Orton and Karl E. Weick, "Loosely Coupled Systems: A Reconceptualization," *Academy of Management Review* 15:2 (1990), 203-223.
10. The exposition of dignity, face, and honor cultures first appeared in Angela K-Y Leung and Dov Cohen, "Within and Between Culture Variation: Individual Differences and the Cultural Logics of Honor, Face, and Dignity Cultures," *Journal of Personality and Social Psychology* 100:3 (2011), 507–526. Further discussion is available in Chapter 2 of Brett, *Negotiating Globally, 3rd Ed.* (2014), 27–41, and in Soroush Aslani, Jimena Ramirez-Marin, Zhaleh Semnani-Azad, Jeanne Brett, and Catherine Tinsley, "Dignity, Face, and

Honor Cultures: Implications for Negotiation and Conflict Management," In *Handbook of Research on Negotiation*, edited by Mara Olekalns & Wendi Adair (Cheltenham, UK: Elgar Publishing, 2013).
11. Brett, *Negotiating Globally, 3rd Edition*, 29–30.
12. Brett, 2015, personal communication.
13. Brett, "Culture and Negotiation," in *Negotiating Globally, 3rd Edition*, 26–28.
14. Meyer, *The Culture Map*, 2014, Figures 1.1, 2.2, 3.1, 4.1, 5.3, 6.1, 7.1, 8.1.
15. P. Christopher Earley and Elaine Mosakowski, "Cultural Intelligence," *Harvard Business Review* October (2004); P. Christopher Earley, "Redefining Interactions across Cultures and Organizations: Moving Forward with Cultural Intelligence," In *Research in Organizational Behavior*, edited by Barry Staw and Roderick Kramer (Oxford: JAI Press, 2002), 271–99.
16. T. M. Luhrman, "Wheat People vs. Rice People: Why Are Some Cultures More Individualistic than Others?" *The New York Times*, December 3, 2014.
17. From the archives of the 100 Year Family Enterprise Project.
18. Edgar Schein, *Organizational Psychology, 4th Edition* (Prentice Hall, 2014).
19. Ronald Lesthaeghe, "The Unfolding Story of the Second Demographic Transition," *Population and Development Review* 36:2 (2009), 211–251.
20. Robert Kaplan, "Asia's Rise is Rooted in Confucian Values," *The Wall Street Journal*, February 6, 2015.
21. Harry Barkema, Xiao-Ping Chen, Gerard George, Yadong Luo, and Anne S. Tsui, "West Meets East: New Concepts and Theories," *Academy of Management Journal* 58:2 (2015), 462.
22. Penelope Brown and Stephen C. Levinson, *Politeness: Some Universals in Language Usage* (Cambridge: Cambridge University Press, 1987), 66.
23. Adam Taylor, "Why 'Nut Rage' Is Such a Big Deal in South Korea," *The Washington Post*, December 12, 2014.
24. Amy Tan, *The Joy Luck Club* (New York: Penguin Group, 1989), 42.
25. Chris Buckley, "A Lunar New Year with a Name that's a Matter of Opinion," *The New York Times*, February 18, 2015.
26. Satoshi Sakata, "Historical Origin of the Japanese Ie System," *The Japan News*, ChuoOnline, accessed November 10, 2015.
27. Cited in Ira Bryck, "Kikkoman's Mogi Family Creed," accessed November 9, 2015, https://www.umass.edu/ fambiz/¬articles/-values_culture/kikkoman .html. For a full translation of a more modern listing of sixteen Mogi Family business principles, see the citation webpage.
28. From the 100 Year Family Enterprise Project.
29. RBC/Capgemini, *World Wealth Report*, 2015.
30. For a fascinating description of this phenomenon, see Chapter Six in Malcolm Gladwell's book, *Outliers: The Story of Success* (Back Bay Books, 2011), 161–176.

31. Adapted from the archives of the 100 Year Family Enterprise Project.
32. *The Godfather*, dir. Francis Ford Coppola, Hollywood, CA: Paramount Pictures, 1972.
33. We are grateful for this anecdote from a professional colleague whose privacy shall be maintained.
34. This anecdote continues the Latin American case mentioned above, adapted from the 100 Year Family Enterprise Project.
35. Navi Radjou, "Clash of the Mindsets: How Indian and Western Engineers View the World Differently," *Harvard Business Review*, July (2008).
36. "Half of Russia's Richest People Are Planning to Cash Out," *Bloomberg News*, November 13, 2015.
37. "Half of Russia's Richest People," *Bloomberg News*, 2015.
38. Dennis T. Jaffe and James Grubman, "Acquirers' and Inheritors' Dilemma: Discovering Life Purpose and Building Personal Identity in the Presence of Wealth," *Journal of Wealth Management* (2007): 20–44. This model was further developed in James Grubman, *Strangers in Paradise: How Families Adapt to Wealth Across Generations* (FamilyWealth Consulting, 2013) and such articles as James Grubman, Dennis T. Jaffe and Keith Whitaker, "Immigration to the Land of Wealth," *Private Wealth* magazine, February/March (2009), 17–19
39. See for example Forbes Insights, *Global Wealth and Family Ties* (2012); RBC/Capgemini, *World Wealth Report* (2012 through 2015); WealthX, *Ultra Wealth Report*, (2012 through 2015).
40. The cross-cultural literature describes many types of immigrants: refugees fleeing war zones, forced migrant labor, short-term sojourners from one culture to another, expatriates, and those who set out purposefully from one country to make their way to a land of greater opportunity and prosperity. Our use of the term "immigrants" denotes the latter, since research demonstrates they have characteristics similar to wealth creators.
41. US Trust, *Insights on Wealth and Worth* (2013), 9; US Trust, *Insights on Wealth and Worth* (2014), 19; US Trust, *Insights on Wealth and Worth* (2015), 26; UBS Investor Watch, *When Is Enough... Enough*, accessed November 18, 2015, https://www.ubs.com/microsites/ubs-investor-watch/en/still-striving.html.
42. We respect that, in some cultures, the term "natives" refers to indigenous or aboriginal peoples in contrast to later settlers who arrive from other lands. For readers from those cultures, we suggest the use of the term "natural-born citizens" for inhabitants born and raised in a country rather than inhabitants who migrate in from elsewhere.
43. For a full explanation of Independence and Interdependence, see Grubman, *Strangers in Paradise*, 119–178.

44. Timothy G. Habbershon and Mary L. Williams, "A Resource Based Framework for Assessing the Strategic Advantages of Family Firms," *Family Business Review* 12:1 (1999), 1–25.
45. For an excellent discussion of the succession challenges in Asian family enterprises, see Ivan Lansberg and Kelin Gersick, *Tradition and Adaptation in Chinese Family Enterprises: Facing the Challenge of Continuity* (HSBC Private Bank, 2009). Available from OCLC WorldCat (www.worldcat.org).
46. Chrystia Freeland, "The Rise of the New Global Elite," *The Atlantic Monthly*, January/February, 2011.
47. Most discussion of this phenomenon has centered on its development as a result of wealth inequality in various developed or developing nations. There are multiple viewpoints about whether the rise of this culture is helpful, harmful, inevitable, or apocalyptic. While acknowledging the complex issues surrounding how many people can get there or whether more of society should be able to make the journey, we leave that discussion to others. We are more focused on who inhabits the ambicultural blend populated by successful families and the impact on family dynamics when one generation becomes more comfortable than another with its perspectives.
48. Barkema et al., "West Meets East," 2015, 460–479; LatinWorks, *The Plus Identity*.
49. Maddy Janssens and Jeanne Brett, "Cultural Intelligence in Global Teams: A Fusion Model of Collaboration," *Group and Organization Management* 30:1 (2006), 124–152.
50. Freeland, "The Rise of the New Global Elite," 2012.
51. Dinah Eng, "How a Family of Refugees Turned a Bakery into a Dessert Powerhouse," *Fortune*, May 24, 2015; Dennis Jaffe, "Investing in the American Dream," *Family Business* Winter (2006), 24–30.
52. From the 100 Year Family Enterprise Project.
53. This case was adapted from Jeremy Cheng and Kevin Au, *Luen Thai: Governance for the Tans' Shared Future* (Coutts & Co, 2013) and from personal discussions.
54. Cheng and Au, *Luen Thai*, 2013.
55. We thank Jeanne Brett of the Northwestern University Kellogg School of Management for this insight.
56. From the findings of the 100 Year Family Enterprise Project.
57. Jasper Copping, "Feud That Has Torn Apart Family behind Luxury Hotels," *The Telegraph*, November 17, 2013.
58. "Father 'Deeply Ashamed' of Radisson Blue Hotel Millionaire Son Who Won't Share Wealth," *The Telegraph*, November 25, 2013.
59. "Father Deeply Ashamed," *The Telegraph*, 2013.

60. James Coutre and Maya Prabhu, "Philanthropy: More than Money." Case study presented at the Family Firm Institute Global Conference, Washington DC, October 8–11, 2014.
61. Roger Fisher and William Ury, *Getting to Yes: Negotiating Agreement without Giving In* (US: Penguin Books, 1991); Roger Fisher and William Ury, *Getting to Yes: Negotiating Agreement Without Giving In*, edited by Bruce Patton (US: Penguin Books, 2011).
62. The Harvard Program on Negotiation is an excellent resource that provides written and video resources as well as various training programs. It also can be integrated with the family business programs sponsored by the Harvard Business School. See for example the article by John Davis and Deepak Malhotra, "Five Steps to Better Family Negotiations," *Harvard Business School Working Knowledge* (2007).
63. Albert O. Hirschman, *Exit, Voice and Loyalty: Responses to Declines in Firms, Organizations and States.* (Cambridge: Harvard University Press, 1970).
64. We thank our esteemed colleague Christian Stewart for his contribution of this excellent anecdote.
65. "Separating the people from the problem" arose in the original Fisher and Ury exposition of interest-based negotiation but is now recognized as more complicated than first described.
66. We offer these statements for clarification purposes for the reader. We acknowledge that expecting an Honor or Harmony patriarch to admit emotionally-laden interests with such directness may be unrealistic. A patriarch is likely to feel he would lose respect just by saying these words out loud to his son. A Harmony patriarch would certainly believe he would lose face admitting these feelings. It may be more realistic that third parties in such negotiations would be able to voice emotional issues to the relevant family members, thereby building understanding while preserving face or reputation for each party.
67. Visit www.dennisjaffe.com for description and ordering information for the Values Edge cards.
68. For discussion about advisors' biases for or against wealth-creators, inheritors, or in-laws, see James Grubman and Dennis Jaffe, "Client Relationships and Family Dynamics: Competencies and Services Necessary for Truly Integrated Wealth Management," *Journal of Wealth Management* Summer (2010), 16–31.
69. We want to acknowledge our long-time colleague David Bork for developing and sharing the concept of a "culture coach."
70. This story comes from Jay Hughes, one of the pioneers of working across cultures as a professional advisor to families.

71. Michael Sanger, "Recruiting Across Cultures: One Size Does Not Fit All," May 12, 2015. Accessed November 18, 2015, https://www.recruiter.com/i/recruiting-across-cultures-one-size-does-not-fit-all/.
72. See the many excellent blogs and teaching materials at the Harvard Law School Program on Negotiation, as well as Brett, *Negotiating Globally, 3rd Edition,* 2014.
73. Grubman, *Strangers in Paradise,* 2013.

About the Authors

DENNIS T. JAFFE PH.D. has been a leading architect of the field of family enterprise consulting. He has helped hundreds of families overcome personal and organizational challenges in the successful transfer of businesses, wealth, values, and legacies across generations.

As an organizational consultant and psychologist, Dennis has written a series of books that guide members of family enterprises, including *Stewardship in Your Family Enterprise: Developing Responsible Leadership Across Generations*, *Working with the Ones You Love: Building a Successful Family Business* and *Working with Family Businesses: A Guide for Professional Advisors*. He is the creator of **The Values Edge**, an assessment tool that allows families to create personal and family values pyramids, and the **Family Enterprise Assessment Tool**, an online assessment where multigenerational business families can compare perspectives on ten competencies to understand their family dynamics and enterprise.

Dennis is spearheading a study of successful multigenerational global family enterprises as a member of Wise Counsel Research Associates. His work has been summarized in several working papers including *Good Fortune: Building a Hundred Year Family Enterprise* and *Releasing the Potential of the Rising Generation* (available on Amazon). A prominent member of the Family Firm Institute (FFI) since its inception, Dennis was recognized in 2006 with the prestigious Richard Beckhard Award for his contributions to FFI and the field. He was also named Thinker in Residence in 2007 for South Australia, helping the region design a strategic plan for the future of Australian entrepreneurial and family businesses. His global insights have led to teaching and consulting engagements in the Middle East, Asia, Latin America, and Europe. He is currently part of the Polaris team working with the Family Business Network to create a roadmap for family and business sustainability.

Dennis was Professor of Organizational Systems and Psychology for 35 years at Saybrook University, where he is now professor emeritus. He has been a frequent contributor to journals and periodicals such as *Families in Business, Private Wealth* magazine, *Journal of Wealth Management*, and *Worth* magazine. His work has been featured in *Inc.* magazine, *Entrepreneur, Time* and *The Wall Street Journal*.

Dennis received his B.A. in Philosophy, M.A. in Management and Ph.D. in Sociology from Yale University. He currently lives in San Francisco, CA, where his consulting practice is located. His website is www.DennisJaffe.com.

JAMES GRUBMAN PH.D. has provided services to individuals, couples, and families of wealth for over 25 years. His work with clients at many levels of affluence — from the "millionaire next door" to the *Forbes 400* — has earned him a wide reputation as a valued family advisor. He utilizes his training and experience as a psychologist, neuropsychologist, and family business consultant, with specialty interests in trusts and estate law, family business, family systems, and wealth psychology.

In addition to his extensive work with families, Jim brings his knowledge of the client's perspective to his work with family offices, wealth management firms, attorneys, and other advisors. He has collaborated or consulted with single and multi-family offices, institutional financial firms, and Top 100 independent wealth management advisory firms.

Jim is the author of *Strangers in Paradise: How Families Adapt to Wealth Across Generations*, an innovative explanation of the many paths individuals and families take in coping with wealth. His work has been discussed in Malcolm Gladwell's 2013 book, *David and Goliath*, and has been featured in *The Wall Street Journal, Business Week, CNBC, The New York Times, The Boston Globe,* and *Private Wealth* magazine. He has published widely in the *Journal of Wealth Management, Journal of Financial Planning, Private Wealth Magazine,* and other media. He is also a collaborator on the Hundred Year Family Enterprise Project directed by Wise Counsel Research.

A dynamic sought-after speaker, Jim has presented at national and international conferences in wealth, psychology, estate planning, and wealth management. He has provided advisor education and training resources for the online educational services of State Street Global Advisors along with webinars for such organizations as Fidelity Family Office Services and the Family Office Exchange. As a faculty member of the McCallum Graduate School of Business at Bentley University

(2004 through 2008), Jim developed and taught the first graduate-level-only course in the United States about the psychological aspects of financial planning and advising. He serves on the editorial advisory board for the *Journal of Financial Therapy*.

Jim is a Fellow of the Family Firm Institute. He is a full member of the Boston Estate Planning Council and is one of only two US psychologists in the internationally-based Society of Trust and Estate Practitioners (STEP).

Jim has a master's degree in psychopharmacology from the University of Michigan and a Ph.D. in psychology from the University of Vermont. He is a licensed psychologist in Massachusetts where his practice, FamilyWealth Consulting, is based. *Website*: www.JamesGrubman.com

Made in the USA
Columbia, SC
17 August 2020